The Teaching for Social Justice Series

William Ayers—Series Editor
Therese Quinn—Associate Series Editor

Editorial Board: Hal Adams, Barbara Bowman, Lisa Delpit, Michelle Fine, Maxine Greene,
Caroline Heller, Annette Henry, Asa Hilliard, Rashid Khalidi, Gloria Ladson-Billings, Charles Payne,
Mark Perry, Luis Rodriguez, Jonathan Silin, William Watkins

Crossing Boundaries— Teaching and Learning with Urban Youth

Valerie Kinloch

FOREWORD BY
SHIRLEY BRICE HEATH

Teachers College
Columbia University
New York and London

Published by Teachers College Press, 1234 Amsterdam Avenue, New York, NY
10027

Library of Congress Cataloging-in-Publication Data

Kinloch, Valerie, 1974–
  Crossing boundaries—teaching and learning with urban youth / Valerie Kinloch ;
Foreword by Shirley Brice Heath.
    pages cm. — (The teaching for social justice series)
Includes bibliographical references and index.
ISBN 978-0-8077-5294-4 (pbk. : alk. paper);
ISBN 978-0-8077-5295-1 (hardcover : alk. paper)
1. Education, Urban—Social aspects—United States. 2. Literacy—Social aspects—
United States. 3. Minorities—Education—United States. 4. Effective teaching—
United States. I. Title.
LC5131.K56 2012
370.9173'2—dc23

                                                                    2011047431

ISBN 978-0-8077-5294-4 (paperback)
ISBN 978-0-8077-5295-1 (hardcover)

Printed on acid-free paper

Manufactured in the United States of America

19 18 17 16 15 14 13 12   8 7 6 5 4 3 2 1

To those who struggle against expectations,
whatever they may be.

Contents

Series Foreword

Schools serve society; society is reflected in its schools. Schools are in fact microcosms of the societies in which they're embedded, and every school is both mirror of and window into a specific social order. If one understands the schools, one can see the whole of society; if one fully grasps the intricacies of society, one will know something about how its schools are organized.

In a totalitarian society schools are built for obedience and conformity; in a kingdom, schools teach fealty and loyalty to the crown; under apartheid, schools inculcate that privilege and oppressions are distributed along the color line. These schools might be "excellent" by some measures, but whatever else is taught—math or music, literature or science—the insistent curriculum under all else is the big lessons of how to function here and now: German schools in the middle of the 20th century produced excellent scientists and athletes and artists and intellectuals, and they also produced obedience and conformity, moral blindness and easy agreement, obtuse patriotism, and a willingness to give orders that led to furnaces.

In an authentic democracy, schools would aim for something entirely different: a commitment to free inquiry, questioning, and participation; a push for access and equity and simple fairness; a curriculum that encouraged independent thought and judgment; a standard of full recognition of the humanity of each individual. In other words, schools in a vibrant democracy would put the highest priority on the creation of free people geared toward enlightenment and liberation.

When the aim of education is the absorption of facts, learning becomes exclusively and exhaustively selfish, and there is no obvious social motive for learning. The measure of success is always a competitive one—it's about comparing results and sorting people into winners and losers. People are turned against one another, and every difference becomes a potential deficit. Getting ahead of others is the primary goal in such places, and mutual assistance, which can be so natural, is severely restricted or banned. On the other hand, where active work is the order of the day, helping others is not a form of charity, something that impoverishes both recipient and benefactor.

Rather, a spirit of open communication, interchange, and analysis becomes commonplace, and there's a recognition that the people you're trying to help know better. Of course, in these places there is a certain natural disorder, a certain amount of anarchy and chaos, as there is in any busy workshop. But there is a deeper discipline at work, the discipline of getting things done and learning through life, and there is an appreciation of knowledge as an inherently public good—something that can be reproduced at little or no cost, and unlike commodities, when it is given away, no one has any less of it. In a flourishing democracy, knowledge would be shared without any reservation or restrictions whatsoever.

The education we're accustomed to is simply a caricature—it's neither authentically nor primarily about full human development. Why, for example, is education thought of as only kindergarten through 12th grade, or kindergarten through university? Why does education occur only early in life? Why is there a point in our lives when we no longer think we need education? Why, again, is there a hierarchy of teacher over students? Why are there grades and grade levels? Why does attendance matter? Why is punctuality valuable? Why, indeed, do we think of a productive and a service sector in our society, with education designated as a service activity? Why is education separate from production?

The development of free people in a free society—this is the central goal of teaching for social justice. This means teaching toward freedom and democracy, and it's based on a common faith in the incalculable value of every human being; it assumes that the fullest development of all is the condition for the full development of each, and, conversely, that the fullest development of each is the condition for the full development of all. One traditional way of expressing this ideal is this: Whatever the wisest and most privileged parents in a democracy want for their kids becomes the standard for what we as a community want for all of our children.

The democratic ideal has policy implications, of course, but is deeply implicated as well in questions of teaching and curriculum. We expect schools in a democratic society to be defined by a spirit of cooperation, inclusion, and full participation, places that honor diversity while building unity. Schools in a democracy resist the overspecialization of human activity; the separation of the intellectual from the manual; the head from the hand; and the heart from the brain, the creative, and the functional. The standard is fluidity of function, the variation of work and capacity, the mobilization of intelligence and creativity and initiative and work in all directions.

While many of us long for teaching as something transcendent and powerful and free, we find ourselves too often locked in situations that reduce teaching to a kind of glorified clerking, passing along a curriculum of received wisdom and predigested bits of information. A fundamental choice and challenge for teachers, then, is this: to acquiesce to the machinery of control, or to take a stand with our students in a search for meaning and a journey of transformation. To teach obedience and conformity, or to teach its polar opposite: initiative and imagination, curiosity and questioning, the capacity to name the world; to identify the obstacles to your full humanity; and the courage to act upon whatever the known demands. On the side of a liberating and humanizing education is a pedagogy of questioning, an approach that opens rather than closes the prosy process of thinking, comparing, reasoning, perspective-taking, and dialogue. It demands something upending and revolutionary from students and teachers alike: Repudiate your place in the pecking order, it urges, remove that distorted, congenial mask of compliance. *You must change.*

A generous approach to teaching grounds itself in cherishing happiness, respecting reason, and—fundamentally—honoring each human life as sacred and not duplicable. Clarity about classrooms is not based on being able to answer every dilemma or challenge or conundrum that presents itself, but flows rather from seeing classroom life as a work-in-progress—contingent, dynamic, in-the-making, unfinished, always reaching for something more. The ethical core of teaching is about creating hope in students. Because the future is unknown, optimism is simply dreaming, pessimism merely a dreary turn of mind. Hopefulness, on the other hand, is a political and moral choice based on the fact that history is still in-the-making, each of us necessarily a work-in-progress, and the future entirely unknown and unknowable. Teaching for social justice provides images of possibility—*It can all change!*—and in that way rekindles hope.

A robust, humanistic education for today can draw on the diverse threads spun by our freedom-seeking foremothers and forefathers. We begin by embracing the importance of dialogue with one another, and dialogue, as well, with a rich and varied past and a dynamic, unfolding future. Dialogue is both the most hopeful and the most dangerous pedagogical practice, for in dialogue our own dogmas and certainties must be held in abeyance, must be subject to scrutiny, and there will be, to be sure, inevitable mistakes and misunderstandings. But the promise remains that if we unlock the wisdom in the room, if we face one another without masks and as the best we can be, we each might contribute a bit, and we each might learn something powerful and new.

The core lessons of a liberating education—an education for participation, engagement, and democracy—are these: Each human being is unique and of incalculable value, and we each have a mind of our own; we are all works-in-progress swimming through a dynamic history in-the-making toward an uncertain and indeterminate shore; we can choose to join with others and act on our own judgments and in our own freedom; human enlightenment and liberation are always the result of thoughtful action.

There are a series of contradictions in these propositions that must somehow be embraced, and not fled from: a focus on changing oneself, and a focus on engagement and change within a community; a concern with the individual, and a concern with the group; the demands of self-activity and self-education, and the location of that self within the social surround. An emphasis on the needs and interests of each individual must become co-primary with faith in a kind of robust public that can and must be created. To be exclusively child-centered, to the extent that the needs of the community are ignored or erased, is to develop a kind of fatalistic narcissism, or, too often, a performance of whiteness; to honor the group while ignoring the needs of the individual is to destroy any authentic possibility of freedom. The challenge is to somehow hold on to the spirit of the old saying, "I am because we are, and we are because I am."

Education is an arena of struggle as well as hope: struggle because it stirs in us the need to look at the world anew, to question what we have created, to wonder what is worthwhile for human beings to know and experience; and hope because we gesture toward the future, toward the impending, toward the coming of the new. Education is where we ask how we might engage, enlarge, and change our lives, and it is, then, where we confront our dreams and fight our notions of the good life, where we try to comprehend, apprehend, or possibly even transform the world. Education is contested space, a natural site of conflict—sometimes restrained, other times in full eruption—over questions of justice.

William C. Ayers
Therese Quinn

Foreword

Much has been written about the function of storytelling and the need we as humans have to keep our stories going. We continue to tell and to listen in many ways. Adolescents jointly build their stories in overlapping familiar bits of their lives pitched in first by one speaker and then by another. As the layering goes on, listeners affirm the storytelling with laughter, exclamations of support, questions seeking connection, and occasional denials of "that's not the way it was, really." Adults, too, eternally generate their stories, alternately agreeing on and objecting to the idea that each account carries only a slight variation on stories told over generations.

This is a book of stories told by adolescents and adults about teaching and learning. Yet these stories do not keep the usual roles within such stories straight. Reversals of roles mark these twisting, twirling stories: teacher becoming student of her students while the learning students in her class take up teacherly positions. Puzzlement, wonder, curiosity, disruption, and distress mark the emotions of all the storytellers here. Their tales hold off endings by keeping the stories of learning, resisting, revealing, remonstrating, scolding, guiding, and scaffolding going; there is no end to these tales for all the learners—teacher and students.

The primary function of narratives in our lives is just this: to keep the plot line from coming to an end, thereby sustaining the dual sense of familiarity and suspense.

Readers will find in this book much to keep the stories told here going. The themes of these tales are sure to stimulate readers to generate stories of their own—some confirming, others denying. Three themes run through these stories. Primary among these is the restoration of the need for teachers to learn to take the role of learner and to do so by admitting into their lives the need to know. Supporting this first theme is the idea that disruption and digression promote the will and need to learn. Though not titled as such, the third theme of this book is the power of deliberative discourse in support of democratic exchange.

The role reversals of the book will, no doubt, distress and disturb readers, particularly those preparing to become teachers. They will ask how their time in higher education can mean anything if they are not to take what they know into their firm positioning as instructor in their own classrooms. They will find in this book much that will lead them to question the matter of classroom discipline and control. They will ask how curricular content is really being learned when so much class time is devoted to what students see as relevant and not to the content matter of state standards and assessment instruments. They will maintain that the stories here suggest that only teachers who have certain personality traits can put themselves forward as willing to learn both from and with their students. Equally distressing to many readers will be the idea that within learning, disruption from what is expected as "normal" or "usual" may be necessary from time to time.

Readers asking these questions will need to be alert and imaginative to find their own answers to such questions. They can do so as they see that the stories here illustrate that being open to surprise and hoping for accidents help move along learning by teachers and students alike. In disruptions to routine, members of the classroom step forward to exert social control over unruly students and to support continuity of the flow of learning that has come to be an adrenaline high for many students as well as the teacher. Student offenders who impede this flow eventually earn sufficient academic and emotional support from others to be able to belong to the community of learners that is building information and skills together. The stories here make clear that students can bring social control to bear on disruptive classmates only when they have been let in on the metacognitive presuppositions that support communal learning.

This book is premised on the idea of "democratic engagement" that brings everyone in the classroom into the role of learner. To make this ideal possible, however, deliberative discourse has to be the primary means of oral exchange each and every day. Such talk, first proposed as fundamental to democracy in Aristotle's *Rhetoric*, depends on the movement of ideas back and forth among speakers toward the goal of speakers' voicing of new and different ideas, hearing alternative perspectives, and enabling collective decision-making through dialogue and conversation carried out in a collaborative frame of mind. Deliberative discourse does not move speakers toward an end-point of consensus or a plan of action. The elegance of it as a procedural enterprise lies in the sense of freedom to speak, commitment to listen, and obligation to raise questions and offer new information. Those who become accustomed to deliberative discourse (as is the case with the learners whose stories are told in this book) expect reasoned judgment, equity of opportunity for all to speak, and thoughtful articulation of arguments. The common good of the community of speakers engaged in deliberative discourse takes precedence over the self-interest of individuals. Uncertain matters, those that have no absolute closure in life's course, are best suited to be topics for deliberation; these include justice, fairness, equity, democracy, and freedom.

Learners—teacher and students alike—wrestle with many such uncertain matters. They often do so under the shadow of what is going on in their lives beyond the school day: family dissolution, cruelties of violence and abandonment, deprivations of affection, and fearful insecurities of identity. These generally unspoken fears generate an unending supply of metaphors and narratives from which learners extract and compare themes and patterns that have marked literature from Euripides to Eminem. Abstract ideas that run through these art forms are those that populate readings in English (and social science) courses. They lie at the heart of the liberal arts: visual, musical, dramatic, and literary learning, as well as history and philosophy. The beginnings of the "liberal arts" emerged in the Western world in the 18th century from those who valued space and time for deliberative discourse (often termed conversation or table talk). The tapestry these arts create gives us the basis for the humanities. The stories told in this tapestry remind us that our capacity to be human (and humane) rests in our use of structured symbolic systems—most especially language—to relate to one another, generate and provide evidence, and sustain a constant comparative frame of mind. By the opening of the 19th century, the arts and humanities had been pushed aside by the calls within formal schooling for control, argument, discipline, and standardized norms for learning and teaching. By the end of the 20th century, the joint projects and animated conversations necessary to sustain deliberative discourse had also been lost for families living in modern economies. Two-working-parent households, as well as single-parent households, especially those living in poverty, have neither access nor time to deliberate and to examine features of their current state through the comparative lens offered by the poetry, music, and arts of the world. Families living in modern economies also have little sense of the power and possibility required for deliberative conversations oriented toward envisioning a future of building information, lifelong learning, and healthy relationships.

Though all of the above and much more are evidenced in this book, readers should take up this volume in the spirit of deliberation. Doing so means they must bring their own questions to the stories here. No story that is worthwhile invites complacent acceptance. On the contrary, the best stories generate tough questions that lead to more stories, enable more actors, and develop new plotlines. For example, readers may well ask of the tales told here: What are the features of schooling that make deliberative discourse such a rarity? What "good" is accomplished when a rare chance at democratic engagement such as the one described in this book comes along as a unique one-off experience? How might afterschool groups and community organizations help fill the desperate need for role exchange as teacher and learner that young people have? What difference does it make that the young people in this book live in East Harlem—a place with a rich and proud history?

Readers will insult the young people of this book if these and other equally hard questions are not asked of their stories. There is little doubt that the learners portrayed here would relish the chance to engage in the conversations such questions would raise. They would want readers to engage with them responsibly and respectfully, allowing them once again to take part in a mutually supportive collection of learners engaging in the deliberative discourse so essential to democracy.

Shirley Brice Heath

Acknowledgments

Without an invitation into Perennial High School to talk with the principal and work with students, this book—and the lessons I learned from the experience—would not have been possible. I will always be grateful for the kindness given to me by the former school principal, "Veronica," the other administrators, teachers, and staff members, and especially the students with whom I collaborated. Collectively, you make this work possible, and you continue to inspire me and solidify my love of teaching and learning in community with others.

To the various community members with whom I came into contact as I got off the bus, left the subway station, and walked toward Perennial, and with whom I exchanged curious looks, smiles, and laughter, I say "Thank you" as if there is no tomorrow. You sent me on my way and encouraged me to keep moving forward. Without a doubt, you are definitely soul survivors and unsung heroes in a world that is too often unfair and unforgiving.

Oftentimes—more than I would like to count—public school teachers get the short end of the stick, having to defend their jobs against public criticism, against state-sanctioned tests, and against those who think they could teach better than teachers, but who have never stepped into an actual classroom. What is it about these attacks against teachers, those brave people who work around the clock, and who stay at school long after the last period ends and the school doors are about to be locked for the night? Have we forgotten the demands placed upon teachers to adequately prepare our future leaders, preparation that does not just happen overnight—from grading countless papers when their students and parents are long off to sleep, to developing innovative curricula that seek to reach and motivate students in critical ways, to having to pay back burdensome amounts of money in school loans? And now, to fight against attacks waged upon collective bargaining rights? I have not forgotten you:

Therefore, a heartfelt thank-you to all public school teachers! Personally, I extend this thank-you to those who have taught me in public schools in Charleston, South Carolina. I hope I live up to the expectations.

As some of you might know, I currently direct a program through the National Council of Teachers of English named *Cultivating New Voices Among Scholars of Color* (CNV). This is a 2-year grant program that pairs accepted fellows (e.g., advanced graduate students, new tenure-track professors) with mentors, or experienced scholars, in language, literacy, culture, teaching and teacher education, and English studies. As director, I have the pleasure of working with, and getting to personally know, some fabulous people whose visionary insights strengthen my own professional and activist work. I say thank you to those who have been and are currently involved in CNV. I extend that thank-you to also include those CNV fellows whose articles appear in a theme issue of *Research in the Teaching of English* (November 2010) that I guest-edited with Arnetha Ball and María Fránquiz. I also want to thank those CNV fellows and mentors whose chapters appear in my edited book, *Urban Literacies: Critical Perspectives on Language, Learning, and Community* (2011).

Aspects of this work have been shared at various meetings and conferences, including the American Educational Research Association, Conference on College Composition and Communication, and National Council of Teachers of English, and as guest lectures at the University of South Carolina and The Ohio State University. I am grateful for such opportunities.

Also, I am thrilled beyond belief that as soon as I type the last word in this acknowledgment, I will be able to turn some of my attention to current work that is being supported by a Fulbright-Hays Award to Sierra Leone. I have the good fortune of collaborating with a group of wonderful public school teachers and educational scholars, headed by Gloria Boutte and Susi Long from the University of South Carolina at Columbia. Thank you for your dedication to this work in my home state! I am so happy to be a part of this important collaboration.

Additionally, I am thankful to have wonderful doctoral advisees in the School of Teaching and Learning at The Ohio State University. I must recognize Tamara Butler, my advisee and graduate assistant, whose emerging work is as inspiring to read as it is to listen to; Deb Petrone, another advisee whose masterful artistic mind and vision are beyond me; and graduate students who participate in the Reading Group (H.A.M.) I facilitate. They are Christy Bragg, Allison Wynhoff Olsen, Lisa Patrick, Cate Sacchi, Tamara Butler, and Deb Petrone. Amazing women who do amazing work! To the countless other students with whom I have worked and continue to work—particularly Candace Thomas, a high school counselor in New York City's Harlem community and former graduate student at Teachers College—I hope you know how inspired I am by your work and commitment to humanizing teaching and learning alongside young people.

I would be remiss if I do not thank my very patient and wonderful acquisitions editor, Emily Renwick, for responses to my multiple emails and for feedback on the entire book project. Thank you, Carole Saltz, director of Teachers College Press, for believing in this work, and thank you to members of the editorial board, the external reviewers, and the series editors, Bill Ayers and Therese Quinn, for providing me with important suggestions.

To my very dear friends-and-colleagues, Marcelle Haddix, Mariana Souto-Manning, Detra Price-Dennis, Maisha T. Winn, Yolanda Sealy-Ruiz, Beverly Moss, Cynthia Tyson, and Cynthia Dillard, I want to thank you for encouraging me on my way and for always supporting the work I do in the academy and in communities. Everyone needs such honest, supportive, intellectually stimulating, and down-to-earth sistas in their lives.

Family is important to me; therefore, I thank my parents, Virginia and Louis, my brothers Wendell and Louis, my aunts, uncles, cousins, nieces and nephews, and other family members and friends. Thank you for always supporting what I do, even if what I do doesn't always appear to be clear.

That special and kind man in my life, my husband, Tom! Saying a million thank-yous would never come close to acknowledging your unwavering patience and love.

Finally, a huge thank-you to those who decide to read this book. I await your comments and questions, and in the meantime, I hope that the narratives offered in *Crossing Boundaries* are as inspiring, hopeful, and relevant to your work in, and thoughts on, teaching and learning. Do know that I take full responsibility for this work and how it is represented here, and that I remain thankful for your support.

Crossing Boundaries—
Teaching and Learning
with Urban Youth

"Miss, You Crazy for This"

Crossing Boundaries and Collaborating for Change

The purpose of this book is to theorize and discuss critical aspects of teaching and learning that emerged within the space of Perennial High School in New York City's East Harlem community. It draws on a wealth of data collected during the 2006–2007 academic year, including audio and video recordings of class sessions, surveys, questionnaires, excerpts from my teacher-researcher fieldnotes, student reflections on teaching and learning, and, among other sources of data, an array of student writings, required and voluntary. Employing a qualitative research approach framed within a critical teacher-researcher reflexive lens, *Crossing Boundaries* revisits important scholarship on educating people of color (Delpit, 1995, 1996; Fox, 2009; Woodson, 1933/2011) in order to highlight the urgency with which to enact critical, creative methods in research and pedagogical practices (Darling-Hammond, 2010; Greene, 2000) in urban classrooms. Doing so requires that I offer specific narratives of teaching within this defined urban context as well as account for the ways students are, and should be, seen as active participants in the learning process. Thus, this book is guided by the following inquiries, which are addressed both implicitly and explicitly in the accompanying chapters:

- In what ways do students in the English course at Perennial enhance their literate identities through critical reading and writing? As they enhance their literate identities, what are some of the ways students rely on personal experiences to question meanings of literacy and democracy inside of school?
- What do students think about equity in education, and how might classroom exchanges on equity by teacher education candidates and high school students be framed in what one student refers to as "common ground?"
- What are some of the pedagogical strategies that can be used to collaborate with youth in communicating, orally and in print, powerful and personal literacy stories on identity, struggle, and feelings of alienation?

- In what ways do democracy, codes of power, and feelings of miscommunication influence, or affect, students' classroom-based literacy engagements?
- How do youth draw on texts to present aspects of their personal lives that are often absent from, or ignored in, their school-based experiences?

To consider these questions is to situate teaching and learning within the context of Perennial and within my collaborations with students. As part of my ongoing interest to better connect theories and methods that English education candidates learned in their teacher training programs with the practices of teachers and students in public schools, I embraced the opportunity to work with students at Perennial. Initially, I entered the school to mentor two freshman-level students, Alexandria and Quinton, who were marked by some of the teachers as disorderly or academically disengaged, descriptions that neither Alexandria nor Quinton fully embodied, but ones that they acknowledged were assigned to them and that they sometimes performed. In other words, these markers were not clear indications of their intellectual capacities, academic and personal interests, or attitudes toward learning. The ways in which Alexandria, Quinton, and other students I discuss throughout this book disrupted identity markers (e.g., lazy, disinterested in learning, unruly, etc.) propelled my literacy work at Perennial. Beginning in the fall of 2006, I met with Alexandria and Quinton weekly, and as I describe in Chapter 2, our collaborations highly informed the pedagogical practices, conversations, and interactions students and I shared in the English course I taught during the spring of 2007.

Alexandria, an African American female student who was in the 9th grade at the time of my work at Perennial, lived in the Harlem community. Quite often some of the teachers and school staff would describe her as "unreasonable," "loud," and "unruly." However, after working with Alexandria on a weekly basis, sometimes two to three times a week, I observed her intense interest in reading literature. From Edwidge Danticat to June Jordan to Toni Morrison, she devoured every book—assigned and self-selected—she encountered in a timely fashion. Her teachers could not keep up with her reading pace, passion, and interest, and often translated her classroom boredom into unruly behavior. In my opinion, Alexandria's teachers and peers did not adequately challenge her; they were neither as passionate about reading nor as swept away by genre studies, romantic drama, and figurative language as Alexandria. She did not feel as if she was rigorously challenged in the classroom, an often difficult task for some teachers to do well when there are 25, 30, or more students in a 48- to 50-minute class period. Additionally, because Alexandria completed every assignment as if she were running a marathon that she was bound to win (that is, when

she felt compelled to complete her work), she turned to reading street fic-
tion, writing unassigned book reviews, and talking to peers whose attention
needed to be directed on course requirements. More often than I would like
to admit, she funneled her boredom not only into distracting students from
their work, but into initiating fights with them, for which she would be
suspended from school.

Then there was Quinton, an African American male student who was
also in the 9th grade and lived in the Harlem area. In addition to Alexandria, he was one of the first students with whom I worked during my
time at Perennial. Quinton was often referred to as disengaged and easily
distracted from course work, and he admitted to me that he was regularly
bored in classes. His reasons were somewhat similar to those of Alexandria, for he felt disconnected from the mundane, traditional, skills-based
classroom tasks that he was required to complete, but which he often
did not do. While he confessed to me that he sometimes embodied a lazy
disposition because "most lessons lame anyway," he realized the amount
of attention he needed to give to his teachers and assignments in order to
eventually pass his classes. Yet in our group sessions, that is, in my joint
meetings with Alexandria and Quinton, he displayed a critical capacity
for literacy. He shared stories of his participation in community events,
his reading of magazines and newspapers, and his success in solving
mathematical problems. With these things in mind, I began to contemplate the reasons why Alexandria and Quinton were frequently distracted
from—and off-task when it came to—class assignments. Thus, they were
labeled underperforming, underprepared, and unruly in light of their in-
vestments in having critical conversations with me about texts, sports, afterschool time, community literacy engagements, and social relationships.
They were—by any stretch of the imagination—critical thinkers, literacy
learners, and, as I describe other students I worked with in a different
high school in New York City (Kinloch, 2010a), soul survivors whose
school-based interactions represented resistances to traditional learning
and rote memorization.

Because of my ongoing encounters with Alexandria and Quinton, I eagerly accepted the principal's invitation to serve as a teacher-researcher for a
mandatory English course at the school. The class met 5 days a week from
January to June and had approximately 27 enrolled students who represented multiple learning levels and had various academic strengths and personal challenges. Teaching the course aligned with my university teaching
responsibilities and challenged the ways I worked with teacher education
candidates and practicing public schoolteachers. It pushed me to actively
speak back to "friendly" unwarranted comments by teachers who insisted
some students would not complete assigned work (in class or at home) and
would resist being pushed in intellectually stimulating ways: "There's Chris-

tina, and she's always giving everyone a problem," insisted one colleague (see Chapter 5 for a discussion on Christina), and "Keep an eye out for Aureliano. He won't write a sentence but'll act out at the drop of a pin," insisted another (see Chapter 4 for a discussion on Aureliano).

Such remarks motivated me to listen to students' perspectives, especially when it came to topics of belonging, alienation, miscommunication, identity, and schooling. I mention these things because they serve as the basis for how I situate myself in this work: first, as an observer of the literacy engagements of Alexandria and Quinton across the entire academic year, and then as a teacher-researcher in a class of approximately 27 students whose interruptions and disruptions of class activities signified resistances with learning, teaching, teachers, and peers. Students in the course, those whom I observed in the school, and those who frequently stopped me in the hallway to simply talk were "literacy learners" (Kinloch, 2007, 2010a) who were honest about their perceptions of teachers ("You can tell who cares and who don't"), teaching ("Some teachers . . . get us doing routine work and that's unfair"), and learning that is not interactive ("the Do Now and Aim"; "book work"; and "worksheets"). Undoubtedly, students have a lot to say about teaching and learning, and it is past time for teachers, teacher educators, researchers, and other interested persons to listen to their opinions in ways that center students in curricular work, pedagogical practices, and educational policies. *Crossing Boundaries* represents one small attempt at centering students and their diverse engagements with literacy in teaching and learning.

CENTERING STUDENTS

When I think about Alexandria and Quinton, I am quickly reminded of the many other young people who are featured in research studies conducted by various literacy scholars. There is Gil, a 15-year-old African American male whose skills in "turntablism," according to Gustavson (2008), allow him to experiment with form and process; James, an African American adolescent reader to whom Staples (2008) refers as a cultural critic; Keisha and Troy, two African American students in Mahiri and Sablo's (1996) research who engaged in rich out-of-school literacy practices; and EJ, an 18-year-old male of Honduran descent who Vasudevan (2009) describes as a student in the juvenile justice system, but who has since emerged as a leader among his peers. These researchers, among many others, purposefully and critically focus on the literacy encounters of urban youth, many of whom feel marginalized within school spaces. Their work points to the importance of recognizing the creative literacy interests of youth in ways that influence pedagogical practices, engagements, and acts of meaning making.

Undoubtedly, scholars (Dimitriadis, 2001; Gustavson, 2008; Mahiri & Sablo, 1996; Paris & Kirkland, 2011; Staples, 2008; Vasudevan, 2009; Winn, 2011) are working with young people who are actively calling into question meanings of teaching and learning in and out of school settings. Taken together, the critical practices highlighted in these studies serve as reminders of the expansiveness of literacy in terms of knowledge production and interactions with learning. In another way, these practices serve as reminders of the increasing demand for educators (and schools) to work with students and their peer and familial support systems to bridge divisions (e.g., ideological, social, digital, spatial) between youth performances of literacy across shifting, highly complex nonschool contexts, and state-sanctioned expectations of students' literacy abilities in schools.

Along with the aforementioned scholarship, my current and ongoing work is also heavily informed by research on teaching and teacher education, specifically by Haddix (2010), Kim (2011), and Souto-Manning (2011). In her article on the hybrid identities of Latina and Black pre-service teachers, Haddix examines the discursive practices of teachers of color in ways that draw attention to their race, language, and identity within and across diverse contexts. According to Haddix, there are "many possibilities that can result from an emphasis on valuing the cultural, racial, and linguistic perspectives that all teachers bring to the teaching and learning experience" (p. 119). I believe the various possibilities—engaging in critical self-reflexivity, working toward equitable pedagogical practices and structures, and embracing multicultural frameworks—will impact how teachers work with students in public school classrooms. Connected to Haddix's insistence that there are lots of "possibilities" in work focused on critical literacy in teaching and teacher education, is scholarship by Souto-Manning (2011) and Kim (2011).

Souto-Manning highlights specific situated representations of transformative teacher education in her study on Freirean culture circles with early childhood teachers. By exploring dialogue in the presence of differing teacher perspectives as well as cultural conflicts in teaching diverse students, she reconceptualizes professional development in ways that center teachers' insights and epistemological beliefs (which, I argue, relate to the ways teachers can center students' perspectives and knowledge in classroom encounters). This centering of beliefs, insights, and perspectives is a primary concern in Kim's (2011) work. Implicitly building off of Haddix's (2010) attention to teacher hybrid identities and Souto-Manning's (2011) examination of cultural conflicts in teaching, Kim turns the gaze on the ways a high school teacher in Chicago, Illinois, creates curricular moments around popular culture. Doing so, for Kim, encourages students to bridge divisions posed by school-sponsored literacy engagements and personal interests in order to move closer toward academic achievement. However, as Kim warns, if teachers "are serious about changing education . . . shaking on a little hip-hop culture will not be enough" in the absence of "teaching something that you are passionate about, that resonates with your students, and about being conscious and reflective about teaching and learning" (p. 174).

The abovementioned scholars and scholarship employ diverse methodological approaches, theoretical perspectives, and spaces of learning to broaden meanings of teaching and learning for youth of color. The chapters in *Crossing Boundaries* represent my attempts at teasing out larger issues, tensions, and questions about teaching and learning that relate specifically to literacy engagements, literate identities, democracy, resistances, and feelings of alienation experienced by some high school students in an urban context. Therefore I reject deficit models that have traditionally defined the literacy abilities of students of color, especially African American and Latino/a youth. In this rejection, *Crossing Boundaries* reflects my commitment to privileging the voices of students who have too often been marginalized in public debates on educational improvement and academic achievement. Such privileging is demonstrated in how I foreground students' writings, interactions, and personal struggles.

REACHING FORWARD

"Crossing Boundaries in Teaching and Teacher Education" is the opening chapter in this book. The chapter presents experiences that resulted from a shared class session with students from Perennial High School and teacher education candidates from a local university. Set, for the most part, in a university classroom, this chapter highlights lessons that emerged when racially, ethnically, and linguistically different groups of students—that is, high school seniors and graduate-level students—crossed ideological and geographical boundaries to talk about learning, teaching, and equity. To describe the shared class session, the chapter highlights two scenarios—students attempting to define equity and equality, which leads to descriptions of academic work as routine; and students calling for collaborative learning environments framed by the concept of "common ground." Questions that guide this chapter include: What do students think about equity in relation to teaching and learning? How might a "common ground" in teaching and learning look, and how can it materialize in classroom interactions? In what ways can teachers, teacher educators, and researchers reframe pedagogical practices and research agendas to include the lived experiences, perspectives, and identities of students in urban settings?

It is important to note that while data from Chapter 1 were collected near the end of the school year at the university and shortly before seniors were to graduate from Perennial, my decision to open the book with this chapter is purposeful. The larger lessons that emerge from "Crossing Boundaries in Teaching and Teacher Education" point to the specific interactions that occurred throughout my time with students at Perennial. From my early encounters with Alexandria and Quinton to my ongoing conversations with other high school students; the principal, Veronica; and staff members, concerns over quality teaching and learning for students in this urban school persisted. Some of these concerns—how to engage innovative pedagogical practices, how to encourage students to take ownership of literate identities, seeing students as readers and writers, viewing teachers as facilitators of learning—were also shared by the teacher education candidates with whom I worked. Thus, I felt it wise to open the book with a big idea, boundary crossings in teaching and teacher education, in order to elicit related ideas from specific classroom interactions at Perennial across the remaining chapters.

Chapter 2, "Equity and Diversity in Teaching and Learning: Case Studies at Perennial High School," presents a picture of the community, school, and class contexts in ways that center topics of equity and diversity in teaching and learning. In so doing, the chapter offers descriptions of East Harlem, or El Barrio, which was once known as Italian Harlem and was home to Dutch settlers, French Huguenots, and, among other groups, African American farmers. From this brief overview of East Harlem, the chapter introduces readers to Perennial High School, which is located in a cultural arts center within the community, and to the English course and its guiding objectives. Through nonlinear descriptions of course artifacts, assignments, and conversations with students, and through offerings from my researcher fieldnotes, the chapter complicates discussions of literacy, diversity, and teaching by highlighting the community, school, and English course as important cases that have major influences on topics discussed throughout the book such as democracy, literacy, and codes of power.

Chapter 3, "Damya's Democracy: Classrooms as Sites of Literacy Engagements," asks: What do Democratic Engagements (DE) mean in teaching and learning with students attending an urban high school? How might Democratic Engagements be understood as a situated practice that brings into alignment two domains of practice: schools (academic conventions) and communities (local practices)? To answer these questions, this chapter highlights how some students embraced opportunities to perform aspects of DE while others grappled with implementing its meanings, tenets, and practices in class work. To demonstrate these points, the chapter focuses on the literacy artifacts of Damya: an essay on Langston Hughes's poem "The Weary Blues" (Rampersad, 1995), a response and writing sample on points from Kozol's (2005) *The Shame of the Nation,* and what I refer to as "a second text" that Damya inserts into her official writings to establish personal connections to the topic under investigation. Together, Damya's artifacts and her peers' responses to them point to the resistances with, and potential around, supporting Democratic Engagements in classroom activities.

In "'Who You Calling a Writer?' Sincerely, Robert and Aureliano," Chapter 4, student perceptions of writing and writers are interrogated. In light of the history of Black and Brown people in the United States who fought against the odds to acquire literacy, especially during and immediately after slavery, there are many students of color, including Robert, Aureliano, and some of their peers, who outright resist being called writers. This chapter, emphasizing the important historical struggle for literacy by Black people, examines how students in the English course came to disrupt their own beliefs that they are not writers by refiguring the classroom and course assignments to support their lived experiences, and by repurposing required assignments through employment of nonschool artifacts and texts. To illustrate these points, the chapter presents selections of Robert's and Aureliano's writings and projects, highlighting how they each embodied *writerly stances* even in their resistance to being labeled writers.

In taking a critical look at students' literacy engagements, Chapter 5, "Cryin' for Christina," poses the following questions: In what ways are literate identities taken up and performed by Christina and her peers? How do these identities mask and reveal academic, personal, and social struggles? What are specific ways students work to un-silence dialogues on skills, process, and choice in order to begin critiquing "the culture of power" (Delpit, 1995, 1996) within schools and throughout society? In posing these questions, this chapter revisits Delpit's discussion of "other people's children" and "the culture of power" to think through deeper issues of power, miscommunication, and alienation experienced by some students of color in urban classrooms. In this way, the chapter presents two scenes that place Christina and her peers' academic realities and personal struggles center stage. The first scene focuses on students' reading and writing activities, and the second scene describes student participation and dispositions toward school and peers. Together, the examples address academic and social conflict in the classroom in ways that highlight issues of power and forms of alienation.

The closing chapter, "Beyond Classroom Teaching: Literacy and Social Justice in the Library Foyer," examines larger lessons across the previous chapters in order to move the conversation on teaching and learning in a high school English course to critical encounters students initiated and participated in within other school-sanctioned spaces, mainly the makeshift library foyer. My concern in this chapter is to think through the wide-reaching implications of this work in relation to, and beyond, the confines of the one course I taught at Perennial in ways that highlight students' ownership of literacy engagements. Such ownership materialized in the questions they exchanged, the types of nonschool texts they read and discussed, and the ways they embodied interpretive attitudes and critical dispositions to investigate current events within the local community and across the country. The scenarios from the library foyer and my brief references to curricular reform attempts serve as my plea for us—those invested in public school education—to include students in our decision-making processes in ways that center them in pedagogical practices and legislative mandates.

Collectively, the chapters presented here represent inquiries into teaching and learning that involve students of color in urban public schools (whom I remember constantly saying to me, "Miss, you crazy for this"). These inquiries take me back to a point I make in the closing chapter of my book *Harlem on Our Minds: Place, Race, and the Literacies of Urban Youth* (2010a). There, I write: "No longer can we rely on traditional definitions of literacy—the ability to read and write—without considering issues of identity, culture, community practices, funds of knowledge, access, and agency" (pp. 191–192). As with *Harlem on Our Minds*, the chapters in this book, *Crossing Boundaries*, assert the need to recognize the varied and various ways "youth are taking a stand, building a new literate tradition, and imagining a pedagogy of possibility" (Kinloch, 2010a, p. 192).

It is my hope that *Crossing Boundaries* represents an honest attempt at such recognition by highlighting and calling into question the literacy engagements, activities, and resistances of high school students in one particular English class. I invite you to cross boundaries with the students and the multiple experiences represented in this book.

CHAPTER 1

Crossing Boundaries in Teaching and Teacher Education

The year was 2007. It was a warm spring day—actually, a Tuesday in April around 4:30 p.m.—at a local university in New York City. The university classroom, the primary site in which this first chapter is situated, was plainly adorned with long white tables standing on T-shaped metal legs, black chairs, hardwood floors, a blackish-greenish mounted chalkboard at the top of the room, and cream-colored walls, some left bare and others covered with poster-sized drawings inked by someone using a faint red marker. Out of the windows that partially lined one wall in this room, one could faintly see throngs of students entering and exiting the building as well as hear the sounds of public transportation—shrieking tires, horns, and car alarms—that filled any possible empty space on the streets surrounding the university. When left ajar, the classroom door, our one entrance into and exit out of this academic gathering space (if one does not include the windows), provided a source of relief from the heat that emanated from the overhead lights. The door also served as a barrier that protected classroom discussions from hallway chatter: the buzzing of the elevator, the hallway talk of passersby, and the occasional slamming of a classroom or an office door.

It was in this space where I taught a 15-week course—among other offerings in literacy, English methods, and research practices—on the teaching of English in diverse sociopolitical contexts. The audience for the course was graduate students nearing the end of their degree program and student-teaching placements in middle and high schools in New York City. The majority of the students were White female pre-service teacher education candidates. The remaining students included a small percentage of in-service teachers, students of color, and White males. Very few students were from the city, and several were unsure of their commitment to teaching in urban schools. This latter point often fascinated me, given that the university, located in close proximity to other academic institutions, research facilities, a historic African American community and a Spanish barrio, churches and seminaries, cultural centers, bookstores, and museums, is known for its focus on social-educational change in schools and communities, particularly in urban contexts. Regardless of the larger reasons for students' attendance at the university, they all wanted to become teachers. And on this spring evening, they gathered together—willingly, but with a sprinkle of reluctance—to investigate roles played by, and ideas that often get theorized under headings of, diversity, difference, and multiculturalism in the teaching of English.

Throughout that semester, teacher education candidates and I examined, debated, and deliberated heavily over a variety of topics, including teacher knowledge and efficacy, cultural practices, White privilege, silence and action, and teaching multilingual and bi-dialectical students of color in public schools. These topics were framed around specific inquiry questions: How can we discuss meanings of diversity and difference as we critique debates on language (e.g., variances, practices, English-Only Movement)? In what ways can conversations on "teaching for diversity" (see Center for Multicultural Education, 2001) include students' lived conditions and racial, ethnic, and cultural identities? How is power defined in the presence of categories—poor, working-class, wealthy, White, of color, and so on—and what are the educative consequences of relying on these categories? How can a focus on multiculturalism help us investigate culture, place, and personal assumptions about the academic abilities of students of color and poor students?

These questions, among many others, sparked conversations on teaching in a multicultural society and its public schools, particularly in light of statistics that predict a rapid increase in the number of immigrants in the United States (Rich, 2000) and the number of students of color in our classrooms (Holloway, 1993; National Center for Education Statistics, 1999-2000; Pallas, Natriello, & McDill, 1989; Pratt & Rittenhouse, 1998). In the presence of such statistics, our questions required examination of presuppositions, pedagogical practices, and ideological belief systems with regard to teaching in classrooms, communities, afterschool programs, and summer enrichment workshops. It also required us to talk with and listen to the viewpoints—cultural, social, community, and ideological—of students (in this case, high school students) who are often left out of conversations on teaching and teacher education in this multicultural democracy. It is Darling-Hammond (1998) who argues:

> For democracy to survive and flourish, those who have been silenced need to find their voices. Those who have been marginalized need to seek, create, and find a myriad of possible places for themselves in society. They must be able to find their dreams in the American landscape if our nation is to enact the democratic dream. (p. 91)

Hence, including actual students' insights, voices, and "dreams" in our teaching, and especially in our teacher preparation programs, might foster deeper, more meaningful educative engagements among students, teachers, researchers, administrators, and parents. In this way, possibilities abound for such engagements to extend across school and nonschool settings.

So, how did this work look in a university setting with approximately 18 teacher education candidates studying topics in diversity and the teaching of English, and why was this encounter important? In what ways did our classroom engagements center around honest, uncensored, and critical perspectives from two groups of students: high school students on the verge of graduation and graduate students on the brink of becoming teachers? In thinking about these questions, I must admit that this work was messy, complicated, and filled with resistances, as evident in a comment made to me by one of the high school students: "You want us to go *alllll-the-wayyyy* from over here to where? To talk with [long pause] who again? Oh, come on, Miss." Indeed, I wanted my seniors from an English class I taught 5 days a week from January to June 2007 at Perennial High School in East Harlem to attend a class session with my teacher education candidates at the local university. Many of the high school students, approximately 27 in total, resided in various parts of New York City, but mostly lived in East and Central Harlem. The majority of them had never stepped foot inside the university before this evening for a combination of reasons they shared with me in words (e.g., "I don't belong there"; "I'm not that smart") and in body language (e.g., raised eyebrows; rolled eyes; lifted shoulders; crossed arms).

Nevertheless, my high school students eventually realized the urgency of participating in this teaching and learning experience: "To be taken seriously," according to Sharif, "we gotta let people teaching in schools like ours know what we think about teaching." As Sharif made this important statement, Damya, sitting in the front section of the classroom, thumbed through one of our course texts, Kozol's (2005) *The Shame of the Nation: The Restoration of Apartheid Schooling in America,* and read a rather lengthy passage:

> What do we need to do to alter these realities?
>
> I asked this question to the teachers who met with me after class at Fremont High School in Los Angeles. "We need our teachers marching in the streets," the teacher in whose class I had been visiting replied.
>
> She had been listening with me to the statements of her students for the previous two hours. She had heard Mireya's disappointment about having been obliged to take a sewing class when she had hoped to take an AP class instead. She had heard Fortino's swift reply: "You're ghetto—so you sew!" She had been listening to students like Mireya and Fortino now for many years. The anger in Fortino's voice was now in hers. (p. 215)

She closed her book, and we all sat there in silence—all 10 seconds' worth of it. The sky did not open up and the classroom ceiling did not collapse, but the tightened body positions (e.g., lifted shoulders and so on) began to soften. "What do we do . . . to alter realities?" Damya rephrased. The comments from students came quickly:

> "Take responsibility for how we treat people."
> "Not only how we treat people, how we treat ourselves 'cause if
>   we don't love ourselves, don't expect nobody else to love us."
> "Stop hatin' on people 'cause they makin' something of their lives."
> "Don't listen to people who think we worthless."
> "Talk up to wrong."

This unexpected shift in our conversation piqued other students' attention, and in order to keep the momentum going, I asked, "What else? What other realities to alter?" Students shared:

> "Alter school conditions—improve 'em and now."
> "Well, how teachers think about us. You can tell who cares and
>   who don't. You know because of the kind of work they give
>   us to do. You just know 'cause how they look at you, treat
>   you. I wonder why they teach if they don't like students."
> "Change the fact that all they think we can do is
>   worksheets and word puzzles. Really? C'mon teachers,
>   that tells us what you really think of us."
> "Everything we saying is about school and school conditions."
> "The teacher with Kozol did say teachers need to march in the streets."
> "That's what we [students] should do." [Laughter follows]
> "You [Valerie] got us talking 'bout all this 'cause you want us to go
>   to your class. Right, Mizzzz [speaker's exaggerated "z"]?"

At this point, students were in deep discussion about the passage from Kozol's text, about academic and public school realities they wanted to change, and about the invitation for them to visit my university class and talk with graduate students. Although I was aware that not all of them would be able to come to the university course for various personal reasons and familial obligations, they all seemed to understand the potential for change that this experience—talking with teacher education candidates— posed.

CONFRONTING DIFFERENCES AS A MEANING MAKING SYSTEM

That Tuesday came and ended so quickly. I remember that morning, rushing to the high school to teach and reminding students to come to the university later that evening: "I need your forms and they should be signed by your parent," I stated. To this, a student remarked: "I'm 18. You got my permission already." Then, other students began to chime in: "Is there security check-in at [the university] or what?" "Can we just walk in?" "Will we be questioned? I'm just askin'." "Where's your class at?" Then, in a flash, it seemed as if that morning, filled with those questions and queries, turned into that evening with teacher education candidates, a few doctoral students, a Spanish teacher from the high school, and, by 10 minutes to five o'clock, approximately eight to ten high school students barging into the room. This "barging into" represented an initial attempt at crossing physical and metaphorical boundaries, which encouraged youth and adults to engage in discussions on teaching in urban public schools. Leading up to this moment, I had asked both groups of students, on separate occasions, to contemplate a fundamental question that is at the heart of this chapter (rephrased here as such): In what ways can pre-service and high school students from racially and culturally different backgrounds engage in critical discussions about teaching and learning, and what are specific lessons that can emerge? As I reflect on this question, I draw on Greene's (2000) sentiments regarding "eager teachers" and "young learners." She states:

> Yet the eager teachers do appear and reappear—teachers who provoke learners to pose their own questions, to teach themselves, to go at their own pace, to name their worlds. Young learners have to be noticed, it is now being realized; they have to be consulted; they have to question why. (p. 11)

Drawing on Greene's (2000) belief that young people "have to question why" (p. 11), the remainder of this chapter offers two scenarios that describe how high school students and teacher education candidates attempted to address my question about how and why to engage in discussions on teaching and learning with diverse student groups. Doing so encouraged them to cross boundaries (e.g., ideologically, geographically, racially) to critique popular assumptions about White teachers, students of color, urban schools, and the shifting positions of teachers-as-students-as-lifelong learners. The first scenario takes a look at how students grappled with meanings of equity and equality, which quickly led to talk of students' performances of routine academic tasks and the need for students and teachers to work interactively. The second scenario opens with a question posed by Ruth, a pre-service teacher education candidate, on students and teachers collaborating, taking responsibility for learning, and creating supportive classroom environments. Her question leads to how Sharif, a high school student, demonstrates academic work that can emerge when students and teachers work toward "a common ground."

Through the scenarios, implications for urban teaching and teacher research in a multicultural society emerge. Specific implications, which I will described in the other chapters in this book, point to an ongoing need to center the voices and perspectives of high school students (in this case, urban, language diverse students of color) in discussions on teaching and learning with prospective teachers (who are mostly, although not exclusively, White).

Scenario I: Student Interactions

I began our class session by writing two words on the blackboard:

EQUITY

EQUALITY

Underneath these two words I scribbled the term *pedagogy*. Hoping to establish connections across the individual lessons being taught to the two groups of students gathered in the room—teacher education candidates and high school English seniors—I invited them to draw on prior knowledge, lived experiences, and specific course texts to think through these terms. In a matter of seconds, Yvette, an African American high school student (not a student in my class at Perennial) sitting at the top of the room, turned around in her chair, stared at the board, and commented, "Well, IN-equality means unfairness, not equal, not enough, and from that we know what equality means!" Noticing others nodding their heads in agreement and shying away from the word *equity*, Yvette stared at me long and hard, her eyes indicating that I needed to move on and call on someone else. "Can someone define *equity*?" I asked, which was followed by a lengthy bout of silence. After allowing the silence to permeate the room longer than students wanted—which was evident by their facial expressions, dropped heads, and shuffling of paper—I continued, "We've heard of schools encouraging 'Campaigns for Educational Equity,' right? So, tell me what this means."

For the last 6 to 7 years, the local university—where on this spring evening, two racially and economically different groups of students crossed boundaries to discuss perceptions of urban teaching, teachers, and students—had increased its concentration on issues of educational equity. Committed to the advancement of "equity and excellence in education . . . [and] expanding and strengthening the national movement for quality public education for all" (University Website, accessed April 2007 & February 2009), the university's attention to equity was commendable. Yet understandings of equity and practices in equity pedagogy (see Darling-Hammond, 2010; Rothstein, Jacobsen, & Wilder, 2008) did not easily transfer into practical terms for the pre-service teachers and high school students. This was evident in their hesitation to publicly explain its meanings in a local or a national context.

According to Banks and Banks (1995), equity pedagogy refers to "teaching strategies and classroom environments that help students from diverse racial, ethnic, and cultural groups attain the knowledge, skills, and attitudes needed to function effectively within, and help create and perpetuate, a just, humane, and democratic society" (p. 152). This conceptualization of equity pedagogy also refers to how students are taught and how teachers practice ways to critique structures of power, "assumptions, paradigms, and hegemonic characteristics" (p. 152). By openly critiquing such structures—institutions, policies, mainstream discourse practices, and so forth—that perpetuate inequitable educational conditions, possibilities emerge for critical, sophisticated, and culturally relevant teaching and learning that impact educational policies. For Ball (2003, 2006), attention to such inequities can result in deeper, more meaningful discussions on teacher efficacy, on the one hand, and teaching racially and linguistically diverse students, on the other hand. Building on Ball's assertion, I believe that a focus on educational inequities can motivate teachers and researchers to better account for the life patterns of diverse students in ways that position those life patterns (e.g., familial/personal realities, social/material conditions) as local texts that stand side-by-side with, and not as insignificant to, or in competition with, more global texts such as globalization, immigration, organized attempts at language censorship, shifting school/community demographics, and the ongoing disenfranchisement of people of color.

Yes, I understand the definition of equity pedagogy offered by Banks and Banks (1995). I even understand Ball's (2006) take on confronting inequities in order to arrive at more impactful conversations on efficacy and diversity. However much such scholars and scholarship informed my thinking, I was still confronted with dropped heads and, for many students, a deadening level of silence in the classroom. Undoubtedly, my students were readers, writers, and thinkers. The high school seniors, in particular, were honestly critical of the world in which they lived and of dominant power structures that cultivated inequality and inequity. Every day that we gathered in our classroom at Perennial High School in East Harlem, my seniors and I talked about the various inequalities and inequities that reared their ugly heads in the school building, in the local community, or throughout the city and beyond. However, their sophisticated, highly inquisitive intellectual abilities to read, write, think, and question, even in their hesitation to name them as such, did not necessarily parallel a fundamental goal of equity pedagogy. That is, they were not willing, at least initially, to publicly build on their critical competencies to question meanings of inequity as agents of social change in this classroom context. As I later explain, this unwillingness impacts their engagements in the larger democratic world.

From my observations of, and later conversations with, students individually and in small groups, I believe their hesitation to address meanings of equity resulted from two factors. There was an initial resistance to talk about equity (and thus, by the nature of the conversation, inequity) in a large group and across racial, economic, and geographical differences for fear of being "called out" or *Othered*. A possible rationale: The pre-service teacher education candidates were, for the most part, White students who "did well" in school. Now attending this local, prestigious university positioned them, unfairly or not, as materially and educationally privileged. For many of them, regular encounters with diversity and difference—beyond a racially or religiously diverse friend and beyond studying multicultural texts in college—occurred upon their arrival to this largely diverse yet economically segregated city. Such realities stood in stark contrast to those of the high school students.

A second reason for the silence may have had to do with students' initial resistance to articulate feelings on a topic that is not regularly discussed in classrooms where teachers and students are active learners instead of teachers as transmitters and students as receivers of knowledge. A possible rationale: This role reversal was a difficult challenge for some of the high school students to confront. Largely, they resisted my requests for them to co-create class assignments, negotiate aspects of the curriculum, and occasionally lead class discussion. Many believed that their identities as students required them to outright resist such invitations. This was a challenge I experienced not only with students at Perennial, but also with many pre-service teacher education candidates: getting them to assert agency and take hold of their own knowledge in the presence of others. This challenge, in my opinion, highlights the historically naïve ways we, as a field, have engaged students in critiques about, across, and directly related to teaching, learning, agency, and identity. Instead of talking about, listening to, and actively facilitating conversations on differences, we have learned to remain silent.

Taking seriously Banks and Banks's (1995) insistence that we do not overlook the critical lessons gained from engaging an equity pedagogy—critiquing assumptions about students, teachers, and learning; dismantling inequitable educational structures—I asked students to offer detailed examples of (in)equity and (in)equality for our next class session. "Provide definitions, conceptualizations, examples," I asked, "because these two words are at the heart of what we're talking about when we examine stereotypes people have of certain students they consider to be *at risk* or *underprepared* or *developmental* or *remedial*. And then at the bottom of that list of labels tends to fall the word *urban*. Why's that?" By asking students to contemplate meanings of (in)equality and (in)equity, I was hoping to stimulate larger conversations in which high school students and pre-service teacher education candidates would come to interrogate longstanding perceptions they had of each other, of schooling, of urban teaching, and of urban education.

Mariana, a Latina high school student sitting on top of a table near the back of the room, asked to speak about the ways in which teachers are trained and how they interact with students, which, for Mariana, related to discussions on equality and equity. She commented: "I don't know if this the right way. . . . But one way, maybe, to talk about this is by thinking about skills teachers got when they leave their ed program." One of her peers, Sophie, an African American student sitting close by, whispered, "Or skills they don't *got*" (speaker's verbal emphasis). Nodding in agreement, Mariana explained: "They [teachers] need to know reality, about how urban schools are, stop thinking we don't know how to read and write, give us more." In this case, the "more" that Mariana was referring to relates to Banks and Banks's (1995) argument that we critique assumptions we have of others as we engage an equity pedagogy, which can result in the eventual dismantling of inequitable educational practices, pedagogies, and institutional structures. In some ways, it also parallels Lee's (2007) insistence that we employ multiple dimensions of learning to yield educative collaborations between students and teachers and to promote cultural learning and academic achievement. Such collaborations, grounded in Lee's idea of Cultural Modeling and her emphasis on learning sciences, can result in student engagements across dimensions of learning (e.g., social, emotional, cognitive) that critique the role, knowledge, and problem-posing skills (see Shor, 1992; Souto-Manning, 2010) of teachers in relation to the education of diverse students.

Take the following exchange between high school students, Mariana and Sophie, and a pre-service teacher of color, Imani, as an example:

Mariana: I'm serious 'cause some teachers just go and give us textbooks as the work and they don't do no work with you [students]. They don't interact with you and you don't learn nothing. And if you have a great teacher who interacts with you and makes the lessons fun and understand where you come from and the problems you face, then it makes everything much easier because kids would learn more and would want to come to school more. That's the way I see it.

Imani: By definition, what is a great teacher as opposed to one who's not?

Mariana: I mean, like, if you go to class and you have to be there by 9:15 and they put the Do Now and Aim on the board—and you have to do the Do Now on your own. And . . . then they give you book work and then after book work you gotta answer questions. And after the questions, you gotta do worksheets and after worksheets you gotta write essays. Now, a good teacher would make these things

more interactive and base things on your real life and have
students do related tasks. And I think that's a good teacher.
Sophie: And you're still doing the work.
Mariana: Exactly. You're getting more out of it and
you're learning from all points of view.

Mariana's statements on how students routinely perform academic
tasks assigned by teachers—"do the Do Now"; "after book work you gotta
answer questions"; "after worksheets you gotta write essays"—points to
Freire's (1970/1997) concept of "banking education." That is, "the teacher issues communiqués and makes deposits which the students patiently
receive, memorize, and repeat" (p. 53) instead of optimizing learning by
"making problem solving explicit and public" (Lee, 2007, p. 57). Here,
Mariana and her high school peers resisted the act of *banking* after years
of performing this act in countless classrooms. Her refutation of this educational approach paralleled her call for interactive teaching approaches
where the "teacher would make these things [learning] more interactive and
base things on your real life."

Contemplating meanings of equity and equality as a student in an urban
high school and community, Mariana was reiterating a fundamental idea pos-
ited by Freire (1970/1997). That is, "knowledge emerges only through inven-
tion and re-invention, through the restless, impatient, continuing, hopeful in
quiry human beings pursue in the world, with the world, and with each other"
(p. 53). In light of the rapidly changing, multicultural world in which we all
live, Mariana's reading of school-space, generally, and teaching, specifically, is
important to critique because of its explicit assertion that "some teachers don't
know us and really don't care. Then they get us doing routine work and that's
unfair." These sentiments are reiterative of suggestions offered by my other
high school students regarding Kozol's (2005) question: "What do we need to
do to alter these realities" (p. 215)? The one particular student response to this
question that sticks in my mind is: ". . . how teachers think about us. You can
tell who cares and who don't. You know because of the kind of work they give
us [and] . . . how they look at you, treat you."

Yvette re-entered the discussion by stating, "that's unequal balance.
Getting us to do things that don't mean much and don't push us because we
minorities. Is that [pause] inequity?" Susie, a White teacher education candidate, softly whispered: "That's a big inequity. Teachers who treat students
unfairly because of who they are [minorities] and others fairly because of
how they look [White]." Yvette responded, "inequality, unequal, inequity
are heavy words to think about by ourselves and to do it with different races
like we doing. Interesting." Her confession that these words are "heavy,"
especially "with different races," points to a larger resistance that permeates
classroom discourse and social interactions across diverse groups of people.

To say it another way, insofar as public education in the United States is concerned, teachers, administrators, students, and researchers often are not interrogating essential questions related to local, national, and international identities; race, class, gender, and economic struggles; and even world literatures that singularly represent the perspectives of canonized White, Anglo-Saxon Protestants. Or, as my high school students humorously describe, "them dead white *mens*." To ignore such questions in teaching and learning is to not engage an equity pedagogy, but to enable silences much like the ones exhibited by students when asked to define equity and equality. However, to engage in such questioning has the potential to privilege the perspectives of both teachers and students—those who are racially and linguistically diverse, and those who are not—in debates on teaching, learning, and knowledge (Ball, 2006; Lee, 2007). It can encourage us to take seriously Freire's (1970/1997) rejection of "banking" forms of education and Mariana's feelings on teacher training and interactive teaching and learning approaches in our commitment to equitable pedagogic and institutional systems. Clearly, our work as a field is not done.

Scenario II: A Reversal of Learning, or Students as Teachers

Ruth, a White female pre-service teacher education candidate, was very attentive during the entire shared class session. She took notes, twiddled her pen between her fingers, shifted body positions in her chair, and constantly raised her eyebrows as if contemplating questions or suggestions. It was obvious, probably because of the "I'm not looking at you" glances we occasionally exchanged, that her wheels were spinning faster than she could keep up with. About halfway through our class session, she raised her hand and commented: "I'm just wondering—if not every student has the kind of stability or whatever, like resources from home, and we're together in a class, is it just . . . the teacher's responsibility or can we help one another?" After pausing to acknowledge students' outbursts that served as initial responses to her query about resources and responsibilities in and out of schools, Ruth continued: "How can it be, how can you help me help my students and how can I help my students help one another? You know, does that happen in the classes that you're in now and can you tell me what it looks like?"

Sitting silently in a corner next to the classroom's entrance, Sharif, an African American high school student, asked to comment. Embodying a critical, self-reflexive disposition in his academic encounters and daily conversations with teachers, administrators, and peers at Perennial High School, Sharif qualified his comments as "very simple." Then he explained: "All your students gotta reach a common ground, you know. Like somebody said earlier, in school it's like a democracy, you know, if the kids have a voice. You can't just be enforcing rules out the blue and expect everybody to go peachy cream about it." Damya, an African American female from Perennial, was sitting close by and expressed her agreement with Sharif's point by saying, "That's right, that's right," before encouraging him to elaborate. Damya encouraged Sharif by saying, "I know you have more to say, so give it to us." Sharif's eyes studied the room before landing in an upward position toward the ceiling. He looked straight ahead as he shared specific suggestions:

> You know, teachers should try to talk to the kids, see their point of
> views, have everybody at a certain common ground. That's when you
> have success. Then it becomes everybody's responsibility to maintain
> that success, that atmosphere. You'll have students who might not
> have stuff [resources] at home coming to class talkin' and takin'
> responsibility. That's success.

Damya softly inserted: "At least the beginning of something that can be successful."

In this context, success, for Sharif, was measured by the ways in which teachers and students reached, understood, and enacted the principles of "a common ground" in their interactions with one another. Specifically, Sharif, after listening to others' reactions to Ruth's question and to his response to it, suggested that establishing "a common ground" could help us to better implement an equity pedagogy in classrooms (e.g., "talkin' and takin' responsibility"). In his own words, "talkin' about, like, equity and equality is huge. Don't force the conversation just out the blue . . . Like at least once a week or whatever . . . say, 'What do y'all think about life?' or 'What's going on in the world and how do you feel?' 'How's life treating you?' Get students' point of views on things and maybe, like, topics of equity and equality might come up and you could take a risk."

It is this risk that Fecho (2004) talks about in his study on culture, race, and language in high school classrooms. He writes, "we who teach and learn in everyday classrooms fail to see the same need to call educational space into question, and, as anthropologists do, make the familiar strange" (p. 156). To do the work of making strange the familiar, Fecho goes a step further to discuss transactions involving students, colleagues, and texts in his search for expanded visions of teaching, teachers, and learners (see also Camangian, 2010; Haddix, 2010; Kinloch, 2011; Martinez, 2010; Souto-Manning, 2010). Sharif's insistence that teachers, and thus students, come to an eventual point of risk-taking in classrooms became more evident as he offered specific questions for teachers to use to motivate student readings of the world and of themselves in the world (e.g., "What's going on in the world and how do you feel about it?"). Such questions could lead to critical, timely discussions on equity and equality (". . . topics of equity and equality

might come up and you could take a risk"). Sharif not only responded to
Ruth's question about resources and responsibilities, but he reframed her
question by considering the ways in which the topics "equity" and "equality" could emerge from teachers' purposeful interactions with students.

In relation to the second part of Ruth's question, "can you tell me what
it looks like?," Sharif encouraged everyone to consider how such questions
(e.g., "What do y'all think about life?" and "How's life treating you?")
connected to learning in and out of the classroom and how learning en-
compasses a continuum of ideas. According to Sharif, a teacher should "get
everyone's viewpoints. And as time goes by . . . people gon' be like 'Oh, I
remember when you said this last week,' and then you can start building
and getting a certain feel of people. Like, you gotta run with those learning
moments."

Running with those moments and establishing "a common ground"
can lead to Democratic Engagements (Kinloch, 2005) among students and
teachers. I believe that such engagements are grounded in critical conversations, mutual exchanges, and reciprocal learning that people have in multiple spaces of interaction as they engage education as a social process. We—
pre-service teachers, high school students, and me—were participating in
Democratic Engagements (see Chapter 3) by exchanging ideas on teaching
and learning. For instance, when Ruth posed her question to the class, initial
outbursts from high students ranged from "You just gotta ask your students
for ideas," to "Well, teachers want to know all about us [students] without
us knowing about them," and "In school it's like a democracy, you know, if
the kids have a voice." With these sentiments came those from the teacher
education candidates: "How should I let you know more about me? What
would you want to know?," "If school's a democracy, how do you see all of
us participating in it?," and "Would you be okay with a White teacher talking about equity and equality?" To the last question, another White teacher
education candidate confessed: "That's what I wonder. I'm committed to
this work, but," which was quickly interrupted with multiple responses:
"You gotta try"; "Teachers put students out there all the time. Put yourself
out there and see what happens."

These outbursts, among many others, stimulated us to imagine con-
crete possibilities for implementing an equity pedagogy in our daily activities, classroom conversations, and collaborative encounters in school and
the larger world. Our imaginings took many forms: using one's position
of power (e.g., teacher, administrator, professor, mentor) to advocate for
quality educational resources and spaces; creating course assignments that
privilege the lives and voices of local unsung heroes (see Kinloch, 2010a);
speaking up against violence and bullying; standing for social justice initiatives; voting; and writing letters to elected officials.

Conversations about teachers learning to help students, students learning to help their peers, and teachers making space in the curriculum to talk with students about the world in which they live relate to discussions on literacy, multiculturalism, and student-teacher interactions. When I asked my pre-service teachers to explain to my high school students Moll and Gonzalez's (2001) "funds of knowledge" framework, Sarah, another White pre-service teacher, and Ruth provided a combined response: "Students have their own knowledge from families, communities . . . that we should tap into and positively use and bring into the curriculum alongside classroom knowledge. It's along the lines of what Sharif said about building off each other and learning together." Sharif, Mariana, Sophie, and Damya, in particular, nodded their heads in agreement. Then I asked my high school students to explain to my pre-service students what ethnographic research entails.

After catching eyes with Rajon, an African American student from Perennial, I asked him to "take a shot at explaining ethnography." Hesitantly, he shared: "Like when somebody studies a group of people, more like a culture for a period of time." Sharif inserted, "We learned about that in our class 'cause we were talking about how people, you know, like from the outside could study something they're not part of over time. They could learn a lot of important information." He concluded, "That related to, like, where most of us live [Harlem] and the things we think's not fair for that community." Marti, a White pre-service teacher, shared, "That takes you to talking about inequality, inequity, racism, and discriminatory practices. It stems from conversations and comments from students. Then, connect that to what you [pointing at me] said before about equity pedagogy and engagement." Listening to Marti's points caused Sharif's lightbulb to go off: "Oh, I see. Then, all of that goes back to, back to . . . what's it called? Yeah, to democracy." Yvette re-entered the discussion and said, "to engagements," and in almost a ripple effect, I heard whispers of "Democratic Engagements."

Students slowly embraced talk of Democratic Engagements, as introduced into the classroom discussion by Sharif. They appeared fascinated by its potential power to motivate students and teachers to have conversations about the world that could lead to discussions on equity and equality, power and justice. However, the pre-service teachers seemed to be more interested in how such conversations on establishing "a common ground" and on equity and equality could translate into written assignments that are not confined within a five-paragraph structure. I explained that everything does not have to translate neatly into written products or mini-lessons, that the processes for engaging in honest discussions on (in)equity, (in)equality, and racism, for example, are significant in and of themselves. Patricia, an African American student from Perennial, provided evidence for my claims:

"That's right. Why teachers always making us [students] do the same writing assignments? In English class, she [Valerie] got us creating different assignments, like videos and books and even . . . *[thinking aloud: what you call what Aureliano did with his guitar]* presentations, performances" (see Chapter 4).

The teacher education candidates still wanted specific practices and teaching ideas; therefore, I briefly talked about the work my high school students were doing. Damya shared one of her extended spoken-word poems and later explained that it has just as much to do with being a person of color reflecting on life as with critiquing racist practices in America. Rajon searched for his writings in his backpack, and upon discovering he did not have a copy with him, said, "I'm not a poet or writer or nothing, but I've been looking around me . . . and instead of just saying the world's unfair for people looking like me, you know, I turned to writing about it. I don't have my writing here, though." Finally, I glanced at Sharif, who glanced back at me and remarked, "Yeah, I got something. Basically, uhm, recently, we had a project and I was just studying like three singers or poets that, basically, state like how I felt and stuff . . . it's been, like, a while since I did this assignment, so I'm not explaining it well."

The class assignment Sharif was referring to was titled "Writers as Rappers, Musicians as Poets," and required students to select either musicians or a series of songs to closely study, critique, and produce an interactive response to (e.g., a written product accompanied by a performance, a student-created documentary, a multi-genre project). Students located as much information as possible on their selection—information about the musicians' lives, the musical selections, the writing patterns and processes that the musicians employed or that the songs represented. They created an annotated list of films, videos, novels, essays, and/or documentaries that influenced or were influenced by the musicians and/or themes of the songs. The point of the assignment was for students to think about writing "outside of the box" of a traditional five-paragraph essay on a pre-assigned topic. I wanted them to understand that writing happens everywhere, all the time: It appears in classrooms, on the subways, on billboards, on television, in popular culture, and in the various ways we communicate ideas with others.

To the teacher education candidates and others gathered in the room, Sharif talked about his decision to write a traditional persuasive essay on the relevance of hip-hop culture by focusing on three well-known artists: Juelz Santana, Nas, and Jay-Z. From the essay, he crafted five original poems on themes that emerged from his close readings of rap lyrics, investigations into the artists' lives, and from his thesis on the power of oral culture and performance in African American popular music. Following his essay and poems was a brief responsive journal entry on his understanding of the assignment and the writing choices he made in producing (and subsequently presenting to the class) his multi-genre project. According to Sharif, "I basically wrote the paper and some poems that relate to music and poetry that have to do with my lifestyle and how people sometimes feel about the pains in the world and how it all connects. . . . " He talked about the meanings of three of his original poems, "Remember," "Questions," and "Because of This," before sharing them. Here is an extended excerpt from Sharif's poem, "Remember:"

> Remember when ABCs were the only problems you had
> Remember the days of Tag and Skelly
> Remember wearing Fila and LA Gear on the first day of school
> Remember splitting .25¢ juices
> Remember blowing Gateway Cartridges
> Yeah, those were the good days.
> Don't you remember the first dollar that made you feel rich
> Remember having a small ass TV just to get a picture
> Remember giga pet and yo-yos
> Remember when your pet died giga pets and yo-yo broke
> Yeah, those the good times as well.
> Remember the days of Pokémon
> Remember when "Step-by-Step" was on TV,
>   which made your family love you
> Remember "Growing Pains" which made you love your family
> Remember your 1st kiss which made you feel on top of the world
> Remember the days when you felt invincible . . . Remember.

After answering questions related to his writing, Sharif talked about the need to remember the past, whether playful or painful, as we think about where we are today and where we want to be tomorrow—"Remember." Insofar as teaching and addressing topics of equity and equality in schools are concerned, Sharif and his peers insisted that teachers make space in the classroom for students to experiment with texts, ideas, and experiences. His experimentation led him to wear an "interpretative attitude" (see Nino, 1996) to craft and present a multilayered assignment that featured his poem "Remember." Supporting such encounters can lead to Mariana's interactive form of learning, can produce creative yet critical writings and readings about the world ("those the good times as well"), and can encourage others to see students as learners who "pose their own questions," "teach themselves," and "name their worlds" (Greene, 2000, p. 11). These things can occur alongside teachers' efforts to locate specific ways with which to implement aspects of Banks and Banks's (1995) equity pedagogy. Additionally, these things have the potential to foster Democratic Engagements and critical inquiry moments among students-and-teachers-as-students in a variety of contexts.

GETTING STARTED:
CROSSING BOUNDARIES AS LESSONS IN SOCIAL CHANGE

Undoubtedly, there is an urgent need for teacher preparation programs to critically focus on the ways prospective teachers and the diverse students with whom they work conceptualize meanings of equity, equality, and difference. In this chapter, I have demonstrated how two brief engagements among White teacher education candidates and high school students of color can help us question public assumptions of urban youth and their academic abilities, beliefs, and performances. Such interrogations, I believe, can lead to critical approaches to working with urban students in ways that do not silence them or ask them to abandon their critical voices, creative choices, and lived realities. It can also encourage teachers to experiment, alongside students, with expansive meanings of teaching and learning in working toward a "multi-disciplinary understanding of language, literacy, and pedagogy" (Cochran-Smith & Lytle, 1999, p. 16).

On this latter point, educational researchers Cochran-Smith and Lytle (1999) argue that teachers are not passive, mechanical transmitters of knowledge, but are active learners and researchers, many of whom work for "social action and social change" (p. 15). Although not grounded within a multicultural and equity framework (see Banks, 1996; National Association for Multicultural Education, 2003), Cochran-Smith and Lytle's sentiments from over 13 years ago get me thinking about Sharif's plea for a "common ground." What does it mean for teachers and students to work from and for a common ground in light of differences and diversities? What can this common ground mean for teaching that is, or that can become, transformative in terms of pedagogy, practices, and educational politics and policies? Might it mean, as Sleeter (2005) describes, that more and more teachers would be encouraged to consider how curriculum that is rooted in multicultural education and social justice can be rigorously taught in light of constraints posed by educational standards?

Or, might it mean, as Teel and Obidah (2008) would have us believe, that it is critical for teachers to strengthen their cultural competencies by acknowledging the influence race, identity, and culture have on teaching and on the academic achievement of students of color? Or, might a combination of these approaches (Sleeter, 2005; Teel & Obidah, 2008) as well as others (Ball & Tyson, 2011; Ladson-Billings, 1995; Lee, 2007) get us to theorize Sharif's "common ground" in ways where multiple frameworks (e.g., equity pedagogy, Cultural Modeling, Culturally Relevant Pedagogy) help us interrogate meanings of equity and equality, and see students and teachers as active learners? A resounding "YES" is my response to these questions only if we—teachers, teacher educators, researchers, and administrators—can learn to openly and honestly listen to and talk with students about perceptions of teachers, teaching, and learning in a multicultural world.

Recall Mariana's call for interactive learning moments between teachers and students, which is important because of its rootedness in collaboration, democratic forms of engagement, and reciprocal learning exchanges. Her call points to the need for additional research on students and teachers as educational collaborators who examine familiar and unfamiliar discourses (Lee, 2007) while working toward an equity pedagogy (Banks & Banks, 1995). Clearly, many teachers are working under constraints posed by educational standards, as Sleeter (2005) explains; however, we can make our practices and pedagogies more expansive. By encouraging critical engagements across groups (e.g., pre- and in-service teachers, public school students, parents, researchers, community members, educational policymakers, and so forth), we can "call educational space into question" (Fecho, 2004, p. 156), account for students' academic interactions, and suggest expanded definitions of literacy for students and teachers in this diverse, multicultural society. At the same time, we can propose new visions of teachers *and* students as "RE-searchers" (Berthoff, 1987), not technicians, transmitters, and passive receivers. The days of docile students, if ever they existed, are long gone. As a field, our actions—resulting from our pedagogic practices, research agendas, and ideological and epistemological stances—have implications for educational research, generally, and studies on diversity and social justice in literacy and teacher education, specifically.

Some of the implications of this work, which I outline in the remaining chapters in this book, might include authoring new ways of learning and authoring new selves that speak against inequitable educational practices and institutional structures; refiguring school spaces from sites where *banking* forms of education are experienced to sites of inquiry, exchange, and experimentation; and conceptualizing teaching and learning in frameworks that theorize equity pedagogy, multiculturalism, and social change. The lessons may be relevant for learning in the contexts of schools as well as local, national, and international communities. In particular, when I consider these possible implications, I return to that evening in the spring of 2007 when my pre-service teachers and high school students came face-to-face. Although we never came to an official agreement on meanings of equity and equality, we did struggle with these concepts beyond the allowed spatial-temporal configurations afforded by one shared class session.

Through students' processes of critical reflexivity, we—pre-service teacher education candidates, high school students, and I—began to articulate emerging thoughts and changing perspectives on urban teaching, supported by ongoing investigations of readings in multicultural education. The pre-service teacher education candidates shared with me questions that emerged after our session with the high school students. In turn, I shared those questions with students at Perennial and observed them talking about "our time at [the university]" and how "we were doing some teaching that night and everybody was game" (Mariana). The list of follow-up questions included: How can teachers teach students and discuss with them ways to take responsibility for their learning? How do students respond to teachers who do not share their racial or ethnic background? How do you want your teachers to know you? Do they see everything you want them to see and know everything you want them to know? If not, is there something your teachers could do to get to know you better? (See Appendix B for the complete list of questions).

Thinking about these questions in relation to studying equity, equality, diversity, and literacy education demonstrates the need to engage in an educational movement dedicated to the eradication of inequitable practices and committed to transcending the ascribed roles of teachers and students. Only then might we be able to envision the extended meaning of Greene's (2000) assertion that "young learners have to be noticed . . . they have to be consulted; they have to question why" (p. 11). It is important for teachers and students to willingly cross boundaries as we critique inequalities and inequities and as we collectively question why/why not. This act of crossing can prove revolutionary for how we re-imagine the position of "teacher" from a *trained* expert to a participant in a classroom of learners. The preservice teacher education candidates and high school students, for example, were shifting in and out of their assigned positions, at times unknowingly, and were experimenting with expanded meanings of teaching and teachers, and of students' and teachers' knowledge production, agency, and power. On that spring evening, we were crossing boundaries as a way to study one another and ourselves, as a way to give meaning to "teaching for justice." Such acts have serious implications for teacher education and teacher research in relation to the academic lives of countless young people.

The type of educational research and praxis that I am calling for privileges the voices, perspectives, and critical insights of teachers (pre- and in-service; novice and veterans) and students, even if those insights appear multiple, complex, contradictory, and divergent. Undoubtedly, there is a pressing, most urgent need for scholarship that accounts for the reality of spatial-temporal differences, identity and power relations, shifting community and school demographics, globalization, and the rapid onslaught of technological advances. We live in an educational and a political era in which many students, especially urban youth of color, are negatively depicted in mass media as disinterested learners. As educators and researchers, we cannot leave such depictions unchallenged, and we can neither engage in "educational" conversations nor teach in teacher preparation programs without listening to the actual voices and experiences of students. What is needed in the field, then, is rigorous research that utilizes expansive theoretical frameworks and complex methodological designs, that is inclusive of a multi-voice approach, and that provides specific, yet critical directions for preparing teachers and students to live, work, and participate in a diverse, multicultural world. Only then can we expect our students, as they expect us, to engage in the world as active, democratic citizens and, as Greene (2000) asserts, to ask questions of "why."

In closing, I recall Sharif's plea for teachers and students to establish a "common ground." In so doing, he, like Greene (2000), contemplates the reasons for misunderstandings and struggles by asking "why." I rely on Sharif's "common ground" as I present various scenes from the high school course I taught at Perennial. From examples that position the school and course as cases (Chapter 2), that inquire into connections between democracy and literacy (Chapter 3), that question students' resistances to being called writers (Chapter 4), to examples that explore "codes of power" (Delpit, 1995, 1996) and student feelings of alienation and miscommunication (Chapter 5), I return to questions of "why." The following poem by Sharif guides me on this journey:

"Questions: Version 1" (A Poem About "Why" by Sharif)

Why is it hard to go to school every morning?
Why do good people die first and the bad die last?
Why is it that 11 & 12 year old girls wearing knee high skirts?
Why are cigarettes legal?
Why is it that many people are scared to be themselves?
Why the war in Iraq is turning into the one that was
     in Vietnam and no one can see it?
Why does everyone learn what you're truly worth when you're truly gone?
Why do people with power don't do enough for those on the streets?

If we live for tomorrow, then why do some people cut themselves, just
     to relieve the sorrow?
Why dudes these days are afraid to fight with their fists?
Why kids are having sex at ages 10 & 11?
Why is the world getting worse after each generation?
If racism is over, then why's there such a gap
     between being Black and being White?
Why the only true love you see is on TV?
If we are all equal, then why convicts aren't allowed to vote?
Why is it easy to get in and not get out?

Why does everyone want to get their cake and eat it, too?
It's been 2 years and why do I still have feelings for my ex?

Why is love easy to gain, but hard to understand?
Why dudes always look for body before mind?
Why can't people fully express themselves without cursing?
Why people so quick to receive than to give?
Why the gov't isn't trying to end global warming?
Why do we still not have a cure for AIDS?

With so many answers out there, why are there so many questions?

CHAPTER 2

Equity and Diversity in Teaching and Learning

Case Studies at Perennial High School

In this second chapter, I examine the space of Perennial High School, on the one hand, and the space of, particular curricular decisions for, and activities within the English class I taught, on the other hand, as "cases" (Chapman & Kinloch, 2010; Dyson & Genishi, 2005; Stake, 2000). I do so in order to question, contemplate, and center topics of equity and diversity in teaching and learning. Where the previous chapter described conversations among high school students and teacher education candidates, ending with Sharif's plea for "common ground," this and subsequent chapters take a narrower approach to investigate high school students' academic and spatial interactions through cases that might offer "insight into some of the factors that shape, and the processes through which people interpret or make meaning" of human experiences (Dyson & Genishi, 2005, p. 3). It is my hope that such a narrower, more focused approach will present a closer look—a quick, but detail-rich *sneak peak*—into the workings of the class and lessons on teaching and learning that emerged within the specific classroom context at Perennial. Such lessons, as I begin to describe in this chapter, were highly influenced by the space of the school, which is situated within a community cultural and artistic center and within a rich Latino/a, African, and African American community encountering urban gentrification (Kinloch, 2010a). From the larger, more holistic community and the school space, lessons that I highlight were also impacted by the course curriculum and the individual classroom space, the latter of which was located next to the principal's work office, down the hall from the music room, steps away from an active guidance counselor's office, and a floor above the main office.

These specific spatial configurations at Perennial, in addition to the absence of certain labeled spaces traditionally found within or attached to schools (e.g., gymnasium, schoolyard, a fully established library, a cafeteria and school kitchen), are important to note, given that students in my class regularly debated about (dis)connections across school-community interactions. Doing so led them to devise written proposals and digital literacy narratives guided by multiple context-specific inquiry questions: What do students think of the school? What types of activities and engagements go on there? Does this school, and what happens at this school, contribute to students' literacy levels and everyday lives? What could students do to improve, maintain, and/or build upon both the school environment and surrounding community space? Are people at the school committed to equity and diversity, and is this commitment obvious? How can we tell?

While there were numerous other questions posed by students, the ones listed above speak to their shared interest in examining, according to Karimah, an African American female student, "how we want to see our school as a strong environment so we can exercise freedom to experiment with different ideas, try on different hats, as we figure out who we are and think about who we want to become when we leave [Perennial]." A few seconds later, Karimah added: "Like, do we have enough skills? Do we know how to respond to people we don't resemble, who go to sophisticated schools getting more money spent on them? Let's be real 'bout things 'cause we know they feed our frustrations." Another student, Victor, insisted: "Okay, then. Look 'round and see what's here, who's here, what's going on. Take stock of commitments to the school, learning, and everything that make us different from [pause] others who don't go to schools like this, who don't live in communities like Harlem. I'm not saying something's wrong with the school or Harlem. I'm puttin' things out there."

As students were "puttin' things out there," raising important questions about school-space ("How we want to see our school"), access to resources ("sophisticated schools that spend more money"), and commitments ("to the school, to learning . . ."), I felt a responsibility to do the same thing, and to do it in front of them. Over time, as the aforementioned questions permeated class discussions and shaped course assignments, I wondered aloud and in writing about the role of students in teaching and learning, and the role of teachers as facilitators. I also contemplated larger, often unspoken perceptions of school and community spaces by those directly affiliated with, and affected by what happens at, Perennial (e.g., students, teachers, administrators, staff, and parents). In my fieldnotes, which I eventually shared with students, I wrote the following (italicized texts, prefaced with the word, "Then," are fieldnotes; non-italicized texts, prefaced with "Now," are my current reflections):

> Then: *Do students center themselves or want to be*
> *centered when it comes to their learning? How do*
> *they see themselves in teaching and learning?*

> Now: Many of the students in my class had a hard time with
> student-centered instruction, with working with me to co-design
> assignments and negotiate curriculum. The following comment
> from Abana reminds me that students in the class were suspicious
> of calls for student-centered instruction: "For real, you don't want

to know what we thinkin'. Why's it teachers ask opinions, dismiss us when we offer 'em and give stupid worksheets like worksheet's gonna come close to capturin' my thoughts on anything?"

Then: How do I, and students, understand my role as a visiting teacher at Perennial? I'm thinking this has a lot to do with me coming to [the school] since September. That's not a long time. They see me, but don't really know me 'cause I'm in and I'm out.

Now: There were many ways to describe the roles I occupied. The one descriptive tag that comes to mind: Visiting teacher/guest/learner/outsider. Looking back, I think I refused the label "outsider," given students' descriptions of outsiders as people who come into the school, make observations of students in class and in the hallways, write something down in a notepad, and leave without ever talking with actual students. While I don't think I did this, and while I hope I facilitated learning, it does not mean that I was not an outsider. I am still an outsider/students see me as an outsider. How might this impact teaching and learning as well as conversations on equity and diversity?

Then: In what ways might my view of self-as-facilitator in class coincide/collide/conflict with students' perceptions of me?

Now: While I know perceptions of self are partially influenced by how one sees (or doesn't see) self in relation to others, I know that Michael, an African American male student, for instance, saw me as "that professor from the hill who gonna get all poetic on us." Although we openly talked about perceptions, I am left with the challenge of representing and re-presenting experiences and multiple selves, especially related to interactions with students and evaluations of academic work.

Then: What do I think is at stake?

Now: I think a lot is at stake: building on/increasing students' academic skills; confronting realities of the New York State Regents Exam; and practicing what I encourage teacher education candidates to do—co-design assignments with students. These things present challenges with teaching, learning, and working within an equity pedagogical framework (see Banks & Banks, 1995; Howard, 2010; Ladson-Billings, 2004).

In my fieldnotes, I also wrote but did not answer the question, "What else is at stake and is there anything not at stake when it comes to teaching and learning?"

As I reflect on my experiences at Perennial, I feel better positioned to respond to the question, "What else is at stake?" by saying: teaching students, being taught by students, and learning to listen to students by *seeing beyond and through* the surface of things. To do this—see beyond and through—requires me to journey in, and across, familiar and unfamiliar contexts in order to deeply critique meanings assigned to teachers and students, researchers and researched. This journey allows me to work with others at uncovering levels of (un)consciousness that people operate under in daily interactions and with regard to cultural ways of knowing. Hence, literal, physical, and metaphorical boundaries can be traversed as people see and engage with the familiar (what we know) and the unfamiliar (what we do not yet know; the strange). More specifically, in this process of seeing beyond and through, lessons about diverse experiences, life patterns, learning in schools, living *in community* with others, and academic achievements of Black and Brown students emerge. They emerge from the perspectives of those who refuse to not learn, even in inequitable, underfunded educational contexts. Clearly, a lot is at *stake*.

There are many other things at stake in teaching and learning. As Mariana inquired in class, "Does anyone think nothing's ever gonna be at stake with this [teaching and learning]?" To her question, Carlos replied, "How about not living in the community?" This latter question was followed by various outbursts. One student asked: "Define community? If you talking 'bout not living in the community where you work or go to school, I guess nothing's at stake for people who just come in and leave right out." The classroom quickly erupted with, "Lemme say somethin'," "Wait a minute," and "Good point, Carlos." Damya took over and added to the conversation: "If you feel something's at stake, you gotta know what's happening in the areas you live, work, go to school. . . ." She continued: "You have to have a connection. Take this school or class for example. There's a lot at stake because I want to learn, I want to graduate, I don't want to be a statistic. I also want to know about the person sitting next to me in class. To not have a stake means you don't know and don't want to, you feel me?"

While Damya raised critical points about there being "a lot at stake" with teaching, learning, and knowing "the person sitting next to me in class," Carlos's question about "not living in the community" encouraged us (students and me) to take a look around the school space and discuss what we know/don't know, and how our sense of knowing/not knowing impacts what we do in our English class. In what follows, I build off of the above student comments, especially Carlos's remarks on "community," to present details (e.g., demographics, history, location) about the local context and Perennial High School as cases. At times, I turn to my fieldnotes, especially from my initial encounters at the school, with the principal, and with countless students, to further paint a picture of the school and community. Doing so moves me into a discussion of the English classroom and course (e.g., students, space, curriculum, artifacts) as cases. It is within this latter discussion that I hope to begin to reveal various layers of teaching and learning with students in the school, which I continue to present and interrogate in later chapters.

A LOOK AT EAST HARLEM AS LOCAL CONTEXT

Perennial High School is located in East Harlem, a rich cultural-historical community that is often referred to as "El Barrio" and "Spanish Harlem." Throughout the community are numerous places of religious worship, including churches, mosques, and a monastery, as well as public and charter schools, youth and adult education centers, social service agencies, and cultural institutions (e.g., Latin American and Caribbean Museum, a media gallery, a digital film studio). Within this area, which occupies the northeastern section of the borough of Manhattan, are various apartment buildings, brownstones, and old tenements that are in close proximity to subway stations, cab call centers, major hospitals, fashion outlets, restaurants, and convenience stores. On any given day, one has access to black Lincoln Town Cars (or gypsy taxis) that line the streets in Harlem, waiting to transport people to their destinations in the noticeable absence of "official" yellow cabs. Although Puerto Rican, Mexican, African, African American, and Chinese residents (among other diverse ethnic groups) currently and largely occupy East Harlem, with a growing population of White tenants, the area was once known as "Italian Harlem." It was home to Sicilian and Southern Italian families beginning in the 1880s. According to Mondello (2005), "The first Italians to arrive in East Harlem were strikebreakers hired by an Irish contractor to build the trolley tracks along First Avenue. They came sometime in the 1870s" (p. 3). Throughout the years following the 1870s and 1880s, other Eastern Europeans settled into the community.

In fact, in the 1930s, Harlem's Italian community was recorded as the largest one in the United States. Italian Harlem received even more recognition when Fiorello La Guardia was elected to Congress and then, years later, served as mayor of New York City. Also important to note is that before East Harlem bore the monikers "Italian Harlem" and "El Barrio," it was a highly desirable Indian fishing ground that was taken over by early Dutch settlers and French Huguenots. East Harlem then became known as Nieuw Harlem under the governorship of Peter Stuyvesant. Soon thereafter, British settlers arrived to what is currently referred to as "New York City," but what was then considered "New Amsterdam." African American farmers also emerged on the scene, establishing their presence along the Harlem River (for more information on East Harlem, see Bell, 2010; Mondello, 2005; Sharman, 2006).

According to Bell (2010), "East Harlem's population stood over 200,000 strong, with 35 different ethnicities and 27 different languages" (p. 7). Undoubtedly, the community has undergone, and continues to undergo, transformations associated with a variety of factors: its population size, name, inhabitants, and geographical labels (e.g., fishing ground, farmland, suburban neighborhood, urban community). Other factors that are significant to East Harlem's history include rapid migration and immigration, especially but not exclusively during the height of World War II; the movement out of the area by Italian and Eastern Europeans and movement into the area by Puerto Ricans and African Americans; the proliferation of textile and manufacturing industries; redlining—mainly with housing and jobs—directed at minority residents; as well as urban flight, race riots, and civil rights movements.

A LOOK AT PERENNIAL HIGH SCHOOL AS CASE

Amid this history and in the face of a new history, one that now includes a community gradually undergoing gentrification (e.g., construction of high-rise condominiums, increased prices at renovated supermarkets, movement into the area of young, mainly White professionals), is the presence of public and charter schools, afterschool educational and recreational initiatives, tutorial programs, and scholars' academies for multilingual and bi-dialectical people. Perennial High School, centrally located among these services and situated within a cultural arts center, prides itself on its interdisciplinary curriculum, which is focused on social justice and the arts, and dedicated to providing students with skills to become active "citizens and leaders" in local and global communities (*School Profile*, n.d.) [Author's note: As with the names of the students, Perennial High School is a pseudonym. For confidentiality concerns, this source is not listed in the reference section.] The school was cofounded in the 1990s by a local university professor who believes in connections between arts and humanities, a point that dovetails nicely into Perennial's attention to fostering students' sense of personal identity and self-worth, and enhancing their knowledge of art and aesthetic experience.

In addition to experiencing an interdisciplinary curriculum, students are immersed in school-wide arts integration and are afforded minimal opportunities to participate in extracurricular and social activities (e.g., band, sports, dance, photography, technology). Many of these events occur in conjunction with a local university, through internships at community cultural organizations, and in facilities at nearby schools. Other noteworthy facts about Perennial are its extended day program, which runs well past 5:00 p.m. and provides additional academic instruction for students; the inclusion of culturally centered field trips across subject areas; and its multiyear arts and foreign language requirement for enrolled students. Such rich educational opportunities do not exempt students at Perennial from having to successfully take the New York State Board of Regents examinations (National Center on Education and the Economy, 2008) in order to graduate from high school. Some students meet the basic graduation requirements and minimum score on the Regents exam, a few earn the prestigious Regents-certified and stamped diploma, while others struggle with passing the exam and graduating from high school. Thus, while Perennial has a creative interdisciplinary curriculum, it, like many other schools with a similar demographic makeup in the New York area, faces pressures to drastically improve students' academic performances on both school-sponsored work and statewide measures (i.e., the Regents exam).

Insofar as student demographics are concerned, publicly accessible school data from the 2006–2007 academic year show that there were just under 335 students, across grades 9–12, enrolled at Perennial. Approximately 65% of the students were Latino/a, 33% were Black, and the remaining 2% were White (1%) and Asian or Native Hawaiian (1%). The student population at Perennial is almost equally distributed across females (50.4%) and males (49.6%), and a large number of students are eligible for free lunch (73%) while a small population qualifies for reduced lunch (9%). Perennial is a Title I school, receiving funding for nearly 73% of its students, as well as an Empowerment School, having a higher level of control over its resources, decisions, and services (e.g., professional development, paperwork, and so forth). At last count, there were 24 teachers at Perennial, all with teaching certification (100%), most with advanced graduate degrees (91%), and many with at least 3 years of teaching experience at the school (54%). Along with the principal, there was one assistant principal and two other professional staff members (e.g., guidance counselors, school nurses).

This abbreviated overview of Perennial, a small school in the heart of an active urban community, is important to consider in investigations of local and academic contexts as cases. Dyson and Genishi (2005) argue: "Indeed, one's first task is to get a sense of the map of the terrain, that is, of the configuration and distribution of time, space, and people, and of the dynamics of social activity" (p. 39). In many instances, it can be difficult to get a *full* picture of the context, especially in light of time constraints posed by increased administrative demands and teaching responsibilities of school staff, and in relation to examinations that purport to measure students' literacy practices and academic achievements (e.g., in reading, writing, math, science, history, and with decoding a range of texts). Numbers alone—school demographics and standardized test scores, for instance—only partially, if at all, convey the educative and sociocultural impact of learning (e.g., tasks, processes, skills, and meaningful interactions) experienced by students within a context like Perennial.

Therefore, I watched students, day after day, engage with one another, with their teachers, and within a few specific literacy-rich spaces at the school (e.g., the library foyer, where they voluntarily read, discussed news stories, magazine articles, and unassigned literary texts; and some classes, where texts were available, displayed, debated, and dramatically interpreted). I also noticed their performances around multiple types of texts: the texts of course materials, the texts of classroom spaces, and the texts of one another's (and their own) shifting identities. I was intrigued by how students interpreted and interrupted school space and schoolwork. Interpretations ranged from student descriptions of schoolwork as "routine," "easy," "unchallenging," "formulaic," "standard-driven," and "unrelated to daily, personal [nonschool] realities." Interruptions included "talking back" (see Kinloch, 2010b) to assignments, unwarranted and sometimes offensive verbal exchanges, student withdrawals, absences, late arrivals, and early dismissals.

My descriptions might paint a chaotic picture of students and their levels of interpretations and interruptions at Perennial (as space and with schoolwork). However, my observations revealed to me that students were acting in ways that allowed them to disrupt the normalized discourse of schooling in search of openings by which their social participation in teaching and learning could emerge. When Jasmine, an African American female student, walked into class late, slammed her backpack on the table, and looked at me before saying, "I'm late, but I bet I know what we doing anyways," she was not just interrupting class time. She was also interpreting class and its activities, tasks, and events as normalized, routine, and unchanging, something she came to do with all of her classes. When I uttered, "Excuse me," she replied, "Sorry, Miss, I forget, this our class."

On the one hand, Jasmine's remark spoke to a sense of ownership ("this our class"), one that included, but was not restricted by, our shared racial identification (African American). Over time, she admitted aloud and in writing that she was beginning to view "our class" as a space where ideas were not dismissed, but heard, critiqued, and debated, "even when disagreements pop up" (Jasmine). On the other hand, her remark spoke to a refutation of deeply rooted beliefs about all classes "doing the same thing every day 'cause they straight out ignore us [students]." Over the course of the academic year, I noticed how Jasmine and many of her peers came to re-occupy the classroom space by defining it as "mines" and "ours." Not only was I attempting to question, critique, and refigure the space of the classroom and the activities that traditionally go on there (from a position of "outsider"), but students were beginning to do the same time (from positions of "insiders").

To further do what Dyson and Genishi (2005) suggest—"get a sense of the map of the terrain . . . and of the dynamics of social activity" (p. 39)—I sought out conversations with the school principal and countless students the semester before, during which, and after I taught an English course there. The principal and I frequently talked about Perennial's overall academic performance, as reported in the *New York State School Report Card* and the *New York City Department of Education Quality Review Report*. We exchanged perspectives on issues of apathy, equity, teaching in urban contexts, and youth culture. Our conversations quickly led to my observations of students in the hallways, music room, stairwells, in various classrooms, and on the sidewalks in front of the school. I documented their exchanges with friends as I rode the subways and buses, and as I walked around the community that surrounds Perennial. My observations and interactions did not reveal students who were disengaged from learning, who were unmotivated by social injustices, and who were unaware of inequitable educational structures within their current school and in the many other schools they had previously attended. In fact, their critical, sophisticated levels of awareness, especially when it came to insights on teaching and learning, spoke volumes about their abilities to selectively check in and out of school and the associated tasks that come with schooling. Recognizing such insights motivated me to have focused conversations with students on related topics (e.g., student choice, student engagement/disengagement, teaching, learning, and reading/writing interests).

REFLECTIONS FROM FIELDNOTES

These focused conversations informed my curricular approaches and pedagogical practices at Perennial. Some years later, these things continue to strongly shape the ways I work with adolescents, teacher education candidates, doctoral students, and new and veteran public school teachers. These things also compel me to frequently revisit fieldnotes from Perennial, which provide a more personal look into my engagements with numerous students there, including Alexandria and Quinton—two of the first students with whom I talked. Such interactions greatly affected my view of Perennial as an educational site and my day-to-day involvements with students, while informing the design and curricular decisions of the English course (as case) I taught.

Selected Notes on Alexandria

I met with Alexandria in the library's corridor and we immediately began talking about her reading and writing interests. She's in the 9th grade at Perennial and has "enough, you know" friends, but is open-minded and always willing to meet new people. In the first 2 weeks of the school year, she was involved in a fight, and just a few weeks ago, she was suspended for being involved in a second fight. The first one was with a young lady—at the same grade level—and the second one was with a boy (Quinton). He's supposed to be one of her good friends. They were both suspended, and since returning, have made amends: "We're okay. No problems," says Alexandria. The school principal (Veronica) mediated their session on conflict and says things are now fine between them: "Though it seems like Alexandria can't keep her hands to herself. She tried touching him, and not just him, but other boys, too." I tell her (Veronica) that I'll be on the lookout for this behavior when I'm working with Alexandria and Quinton.

I asked Alexandria about the students and teachers at the school, curious to know what she thinks/how she feels about race and identity. Without prompting, other than asking her to share her thoughts on students and teachers there, she replied: "Not a lot of Black teachers here . . . but it don't matter much 'cause what matters most times is getting along with people, 'specially teachers, and sometimes I do that, other times I can't. But me getting along with them ain't the problem." What's a problem, based on my observations, is Alexandria's feelings of not being academically challenged in the classroom. She notes her 9th-grade English class as an example: "We go to class and we write more than we actually read. I like both, but don't think it's right for reading, well independent reading, to get less than 20, say 30 minutes, and writing to get the rest of the time. It's not like the writing actually gets the rest of that time anyway, 'cause we sit and listen to teachers going over the same concepts and structures all the time, or they read aloud materials we've already read at home. I take English from like 9:37 AM 'til like close to 11:17 AM or somethin' like that. I just want to be able to read more. Why's that such a problem?"

[Break in fieldnotes. Then my fieldnotes continue with:]

From listening to Alexandria make references to her English class, I gather that she knows the mundane activities and routines all too well, that she realizes the value (at least for her) of getting work done early so she could spend the rest of class talking with peers, something that, according to Alexandria, "gets me in trouble. I don't know why me when other people talk, too, and nothing happens to them." Alexandria is well aware of her actions and the actions of peers and teachers, and believes teachers pick on her for being off-task when she's "just bored like crazy bored." After we talked more about "getting in trouble," she showed me her writing—an essay-letter she wrote for English class on the book *Dreamland*. Talk about skillful and amazing stuff! Alexandria's a really strong writer. I'm curious to hear more about her writing and reading processes. At the moment, though, she's consumed with having to wear that unfair label of "troublemaker," when all she really wants is to be challenged "at least by teachers or students or somebody . . . 'cause I get tired having to do the same thing all the time in classes. I ain't got no voice? I ain't got no point of view? Says who? I show 'em all the time I got a voice that wanna be used, that wanna read. Instead I'm a troublemaker. Troublemaker? They [teachers] wonder why we don't like school. Gimme somethin' worth doing. Stop hatin'."

[Alexandria stood up and looked around. Quinton was sitting there the entire time listening. The following is how I interpreted the second part of the session.]

Alexandria asked Quinton about his interests and if he likes to read or play sports or write poems: "Whatchu like?" From his look, I'd say he was shocked by her question. He shuffled a bit in his chair and threw a wide smile at us [me and Alexandria]. "Well, I'd be more into class if stuff made sense so I could process what's going on in my life. We don't read things or do projects 'bout family issues, 'bout how we [youth] deal with losing loved ones. You know, the hard stuff we go through. We left to figure out stuff by our self." Quinton's eyes roamed the room. Me and Alexandria waited in silence. He went on: "Teachers don't want us to connect dots from class readin' to real life. They tell us, read a passage in a book, answer questions, but don't talk 'bout what you feel or nothing 'bout things. They want us to give the right answer like there's only one. . . . That's what I'm thinking and feeling. That's why I say SCHOOL'S BORING."

[Session ended]

Selected Notes on Quinton

Went to Perennial today to talk more with Quinton. Over the last week, we've been talking about school being boring. Alexandria was there, but had stuff on her mind. She was in and out the conversation [note to self: check to see what's up with Alexandria]. We went over how his grades are looking for this marking period. Quinton admitted that he's only passing math. If I got this right, he's taking math, art, gym, social studies, English, advisory, and something else, but he's only passing math. When he said that, he didn't give me time to follow up before he made a clear announcement that went something like: "SCHOOL'S BORING, SCHOOL'S BORING, and oh yeah, did I say, SCHOOL'S BORING. WHAT YOOOUUU EXPECT!" His high-pitched voice rang really loud in my ears, and I just couldn't help but hold onto the word, "BORING." How many times would I hear students describe school with this one word? How many students would shake their heads in agreement like Alexandria was doing?

Quinton kind of just sat there in silence, and I was reluctant to say anything 'cause he appeared in deep thought. So, we just sat there. Thirty seconds. A minute. Two minutes. Then he finally said, "My junior high school was better than this, more challenging. And I know this only my first year at [Perennial], but if this how it's going now, think how it'll go later. Don't be confused. Ain't like I can't pass. I can. Time'll show, but I'm just here right now."

[Break in fieldnotes. Then my fieldnotes continue with:]

I asked Quinton how classes were going and he stared at me and said something like, "I SAID I'M ONLY PASSING MATH, MISS. What that tell you?" Again, we just sat there, in silence, and again, he broke the silence by explaining [here's my paraphrase of Quinton's comments, which I shared with him]: "Okay, see, classes could be better and it's not like I dunno the material anyway. I just don't do the work. I ain't moved to. No one's challenging me. Only thing they got to say is 'well, you do it or you just don't get a good grade.' Going to class learning what we need comes down to getting a good grade. That's what I mean by SCHOOL'S BORING. We sit there. They talk at us. We feel dumb. They look at us, but not really looking at us. It's like they look over us, out the window, or at their calendars wondering when summer's coming so they can be out . . . so they can bounce. I'm being real. That's what I think of classes."

[Alexandria shook her head, again, in agreement. Session ended]

Lessons from Selected Notes on
Alexandria and Quinton for the English Course

When Veronica, the principal at Perennial, invited me to teach an English class, I agreed to, only if the course design employed the perspectives of Alexandria and Quinton, Mariana, Sharif, and Sophie (see Chapter 1), and other students with whom I talked. I knew it would be important to teach a course that centered students' viewpoints, even if some of those views conflicted with my own (e.g., students *only* completing digital assignments and not written essays; students not reading academic texts, but only "street lit"; watching documentaries without a critical, political lens; and so on). As I designed the course, I kept hearing Quinton's voice: "No one's challenging me"; ". . . do it or you just don't get a good grade"; "SCHOOL'S BORING"; and "We feel dumb." His comments illuminate a pervasive problem with some commonly held beliefs about schooling that insists, according to Campano (2007), students "conform to conventions—irrespective of whether it fits their sense of themselves—because they have to adjust to a harsh reality that has asserted itself through power. Sometimes the students do what they have to do to get through school . . . even if school does not speak to their identities or inform who they would like to become" (p. 28).

Campano's (2007) sentiments are all too true for many students who learn to "conform," "adjust," and "do what they have to do to get through" (p. 28). Then, there are other students who resist this "harsh reality" by attempting to highlight what they see as problems associated with schooling: rote-memorization and worksheets (see Mariana, Chapter 1), teachers reading "aloud materials we've already read at home" (Alexandria), the absence of a "common ground" in student-teacher relationships (see Sharif, Chapter 1), and school as boring (Quinton). Although I am not saying that there is a magic trick that erases the various problems of schooling, and although I do not believe teaching and learning are easy, uncomplicated processes, I do think that schools must become places that care about students (Noddings, 1993, 1995; Witherell & Noddings, 1991) and their "intellectual development" (Darling-Hammond, 2010, p. 250). As Darling-Hammond writes, "Schools must meet students where they are and enable them to make large strides" (p. 250). This is not to say that teachers at Perennial are not taking this work on; many are successfully involving students in the work of critical literacy and learning while meeting state-required mandates. Nevertheless, there are a lot of other students who are neither engaged in school nor listened to in class, which is evident in their refusal to simply "get through school" (Campano, 2007, p. 28). Alexandria and Quinton are but two examples of many other students who simply refuse to participate in this type of teacher-sanctioned academic disengagement.

Even more so, Alexandria and Quinton's attitudes, dispositions, and verbal exchanges are clear—even if widely ignored—indicators of persistent problems involving teaching, learning, and traditionally accepted meanings of success, achievement, and engagement. That is, on the one hand, there are some students who do not believe classrooms are safe, welcoming sites of belonging where they can openly experiment with ideas and identities. Thus, it becomes important for educators to "work toward recognizing, including, and understanding the diverse modes of participation that students bring to classrooms" (Schultz, 2009, p. 144). On the other hand, many, if not all, students are aware of inequitable educational structures that work to restrict students' construction and production of knowledge, hence, the absence of an equity framework and of equitable forms of education. As Banks and Banks (1995) assert:

> An education for equity enables students not only to acquire basic skills but to use those skills to become effective agents for social change. We believe education within a pluralistic democratic society should help students to gain the content, attitudes, and skills needed to know reflectively, to care deeply, and to act thoughtfully. (p. 152)

Banks and Banks's (1995) argument for equity pedagogies is important for my work with students who resisted participation in "banking" forms of education (see Freire, 1970/1997). I relied on arguments from their scholarship as I designed the English curriculum and considered the types of questions, concerns, and issues the curriculum might raise. I considered numerous questions: In what ways might I collaborate with students (instead of working in isolation) around the construction of activities and assignments? What hard lessons might I learn from students about my own assumptions and shortfalls concerning students, teaching, and learning? Also, what could it mean for me to practice what I require of my high school students and teacher education candidates: be motivated to participate (and not just show up), wear an interpretive attitude (Nino, 1996), and engage teaching and learning as practices in, or that can lead to, social justice, reciprocity, mutual exchanges, and ways of seeing beyond and through the surface of things?

Notes from English Class

Today, a Friday, was actually the first day of the new marking period and the first class session at Perennial High School I was going to teach. It was more than interesting. I took the Manhattan-bound "A" train from the 209th Street station in the Inwood section of Manhattan to 125th Street in Harlem. From there, I transferred to the M3 bus, took it to the east side of Harlem, and walked from there to school. Walking down 106th Street toward Lexington Avenue, I passed through a housing development, walked underneath a highway tunnel, and then down a side street lined with apartment buildings and people on their way to engage in the business of a new day. Echoes of "morning" and "good day" ring in my head from older men and women on the side streets who looked at me and I at them with a sense of knowing running through our bodies—even if we couldn't name names.

When I thought it was my imagination running wild, I caught the stare of an older African American man. We locked eyes. I stared at him as if to say, "Don't I know you?" I tried to play off my stare, but before I could, he said, "You familiar from someway. I don't know. . . . Way you from?" I replied, "Down South. Charleston in the S-C." Then, I kind of just laughed. I was sort of startled when he said in an animated voice, "Must be Charrrlleesttoonnn. Rigggghhhhttt!" My look of surprise was a reply. "Told you, I know you. We know each other down inside." Somehow, this man, a person who resembled a combination of my father, uncles, and brothers, knew. He just knew! I smiled at him and he said, "Treat 'em right wherever you go. You'll learn a lot."

As I write these fieldnotes on this Friday afternoon, I'm sitting here wondering if I'll run into him again (I never did) after that amazing encounter we shared earlier today. Even if I don't, I can say he set me on a path that led me to look at people and experience places with a sense of familiarity and a curiosity to know beyond the surface of things seen, felt, and witnessed . . . to work at *seeing beyond and through*. He also sent me off to my senior English class at Perennial High School, a place where I believe I'll continue learning/experiencing "a lot." In time, I guess we'll see what happens, what's learned, what's seen, and if I can, in fact, come to see beyond and through.

I finally arrived at the school. Eagerly, I walked in and went to check in on the first floor with the security guard like I'd been doing since coming to the school in September. You know, the routine exchange happened: "Good morning." "Good morning. How you?" "Not bad. And you?" "Well . . ." which was followed by a variety of answers given to me from the security guard on duty: "Busy morning already. Elevator not working right now. I gotta leave early 'cause my daughter sick." And then I responded: "Sorry about yo' daughter. I got stuck on the train again. Feel like I'm running late today. Let me get up them stairs. Catch you on the way out." Then, I took the elevator upstairs—or did I climb the stairwell?—to talk with folks in the main office. I remember heading down and around the hallway to the library to see if students were sitting in the library foyer. From there, I went to the principal's office to check in with her. The principal walked me back to the third floor office to get my attendance forms, school announcements, and other handouts to distribute to students. But more important on this day, her goal was to make sure I was re-introduced to some significant people—the front office support staff.

Now, let me say this: I've been coming to Perennial since September. I've been introduced to the front office staff a million times. Yet I'm aware that this was a different kind of introduction for a different kind of day. Everyone was warm and welcoming. What else did she [Veronica] expect, standing right there with me in front of them? I think they were waiting to see if I'd show up, as I had on other days before agreeing to teach a class. Or if I'd screw up and run away from my commitment to [Perennial] and to urban education, a commitment I talked about with a few of them on other occasions. This time, I wasn't going to be working in small groups with students in the library foyer or in an empty storage room. I wasn't askin' a teacher if I could sit in and observe students I'd been working with in one-on-one sessions. So, let me think about this one. . . . What I think they were waiting to see was if I'd actually return to school and swap my role—from observer who'd be caught roaming the halls talking with students, to a visiting English teacher. I showed up. I pretended to not see the looks of surprise on the faces of those welcoming me. I pretended to not hear the phrases, "Told you she'd come," "What you gotta say now," or "Wait 'til she meet them students."

I recognized the politics in my role shift. I was no longer just a university professor coming to do, as I was asked so many times, "What do you do again? Oh, all right." I was now responsible for teaching a class of about 27 students who were a little more interested in enjoying their last year of high school than talking about Langston Hughes, Maxine Greene, Jonathon Kozol, contemporary texts [essays, music, poetry] on community and the cultural heritage of Harlem. This—the English class I was about to walk into and teach—was a case. It came equipped with space to create curricula, with staff members who were waiting to see "what she gonna do," with students focused on life after graduation, and with a teacher whom students regularly asked, "You a professor for real?" "Why you wanna be here teaching?" and "I wouldn't if I were you, Miss."

SENIOR ENGLISH AT PERENNIAL AND METHODOLOGICAL ISSUES

In November 2006, I accepted Veronica's invitation to teach a required senior English course at Perennial. The course spanned January to July 2007,
and was scheduled for 5 days a week during the early morning. Students
enrolled in the course were on varying learning levels and had multiple literacy strengths and challenges. As I mentioned in the Introduction to this
book, countless concerned, good-hearted people at the school (e.g., security
guards, some teachers, other staff members, and a few researchers) warned
me that more than a handful of students would resist completing academic
work and would not do any assigned homework. Instead, they would disrupt class, act out, and distract those students who wanted to learn. While
I recognized that these comments were coming from a place of care and
concern for the work I sought to do with students, I must admit that they
encouraged me even more to teach the English course at Perennial. I wanted
to witness, firsthand, students' brilliance and wisdom. Thus, I employed a
critical teacher-researcher self-reflexive lens to question such deeply rooted
assumptions about urban students' abilities—at least in this context—to not
perform well, if at all. In so doing, I designed the course around themes of
schooling, literacy, and power. I invited students to draw on the history of
the local community to think through these themes.

We studied poets and poetry from the Harlem Renaissance, activists
of the civil rights movement, and books about historical and contemporary perspectives on urban schooling. In addition, we surveyed articles and
stories on the history of Harlem, paying attention to "minority"-owned
businesses, local struggles, and educational initiatives. Our critical readings
were complemented by multiple writing assignments that students and I
often collaboratively designed. These included persuasive essays paired with
original spoken-word poetry and performances, and multimodal writing
projects on a community topic. Among other assignments, students also
completed extended journal responses on course readings accompanied by
dramatic performances or music lyrics that students wrote, sang, and performed on an electric guitar. Learning, in this context, was rich, reciprocal,
democratic, and multiple.

Employing qualitative research methods (e.g., classroom-based student
observations, documented class discussions, collected student writings, in-
terviews, fieldnotes, reflections of my own teaching and learning experiences) and using a critical teacher-researcher reflexive lens (Campano, 2007;
Fecho, 2004; Michie, 2004), I observed students' active participation in their
learning through processes involving reading, writing, questioning, and collaborating. At the same time that students critiqued negative depictions of
the Harlem community (e.g., in disrepair, in need of gentrification), they
rejected the attitudes of anyone who painted them as disengaged products
of the local area. Talking about their rejection of such attitudes (e.g., adults

seeing students as lazy and disengaged) led us to co-construct the course learning goals in ways that aligned with, and spoke back to, New York State standards for 12th-grade English. During the first few days of the course, we decided on the following goals (emphasis in the original):

1. To be patient with our practice of enhancing and improving how we question, think about, reflect, and critique our ideas and the ideas of other people in this class. (This relates to the NYS [New York State] Grade Specific Performance Indicator that states: "Students will read, write, listen, and speak for *social interaction.*")

2. To be open to sharing critical responses to the readings and writings we do for class, and to be comfortable talking about how they connect to what we read and write in other classes. If they don't connect, then be honest about why they don't. Give evidence. (This relates to the NYS Grade Specific Performance Indicator that states: "Students will read, write, listen, and speak for *information and understanding.*"]

3. To use language to make, challenge, and express meanings of literature of/in our lives. (This relates to the NYS Grade Specific Performance Indicator that states: "Students will read, write, listen, and speak for *literary response and expression.*")

4. To strengthen how we use literacy to understand, critique, and interact with ideas. (This relates to the NYS Grade Specific Performance Indicator that states: "Students will read, write, listen, and speak for *critical analysis and evaluation.*")

With our course goals in hand came other, more vulnerable learning moments. For example, on the course syllabus, I included a quote from Monique M. Taylor's (2002) book *Harlem: Between Heaven and Hell.* Taylor writes:

> All the transformation one sees in Harlem during the spring of 2000, both in commercial and residential realms, has been decades in the making. For much of the twentieth century, Harlem's fortunes have risen, fallen, and risen again with shifts in U.S. racial politics. The buffeting effects of a rising and declining urban industrialism and the onset of deindustrialization also have contributed to the roller-coasterlike ups and downs in the community's economic life. (p. xiii)

One look at that passage resulted in student eruption: "Who this writing 'bout Harlem?" "What part of Harlem she talkin' 'bout? What she mean by roller-coasterlike?" "What this gotta do with English?" Then, one student responded: "C'mon, we know she tellin' the truth. All o' Harlem changin', and we actin' like she lyin'. Don't pretend things not changin' 'cause we don't want 'em to. We live in Harlem, and to be honest, yeah, there's ups and downs, 'specially with economics. That mean money. Money coming in my family ain't got cause . . . we ain't got it."

At this, many other conversations emerged around Taylor's description of Harlem. There were side conversations, directed comments to the entire class, and some teeth-sucking mixed with head nods. I thought this was a powerful moment, and even if it was, it was not as powerful or revealing as the responses I received to my question: "What can we learn from that passage? Tell me how you relate what Taylor is saying to our learning goals and your expectations for this English class." Then the truth came: "Forget the quote. How 'bout we can't do nothing to stop them changes? How 'bout that? All the reading and writing, all the 'let's talk 'bout this and that,' ain't gonna stop what's happening in front of us. Sad thing is ain' like we got power to stop it. We sittin' in this stupid class actin' like it don't affect us. The hell with English."

It was with this latter comment that I said: "Ohhhh, okay then. You see, this relates to English, well, really to learning 'cross the board. I'm standing here trying to note all the ways you're interpreting, analyzing, drawing meaning from the passage, and making text-to-self-to-world connections that, in my mind, are authentic. And the skillfulness you have to do these things point right to our course objectives and goals. And, well, I also know these things speak to realities beyond this one course . . . to real life." At this point, a student interrupted me: "Miss, we know you right. We know exactly whatchu sayin'. But this stupid 'cause I'm angry 'bout not being able to do something 'bout changes happenin.' I don't think talkin' 'bout what we know and writin' 'bout 'em gonna change things. So, the hell with it. No offense, Miss."

And so it was. Students went from being excited about co-constructing the learning goals for the course to being pissed off about the Taylor passage I included in the syllabus. They were mad, and although no one admitted this, I believe they were not just mad at Taylor (and her sentiments), but also at me—a university professor who came into their school to talk with students and to teach a class, only to end class, jot down points from class discussion, leave Perennial, and go back to the university. For days following this discussion, I contemplated ways to re-enter the conversation to address pressing concerns. Yet I did not want to feed the fire, per se, but I needed to do something. I re-read Maxine Greene's (2000) book, *Releasing the Imagination: Essays on Education, the Arts, and Social Change,* and when I arrived at "Chapter Nine—Teaching for Openings," I felt as if I had a direction. Greene writes: "But then I think of how much beginnings have to do with freedom, how much disruption has to do with consciousness and the awareness of possibility that has so much to do with teaching other human beings." She continues: "And I think that if I and other teachers truly want to provoke our students to break through the limits of the conventional and the taken for granted, we ourselves have to experience breaks with what has been established in our own lives; we have to keep arousing ourselves to begin again" (p. 109).

From Greene's text, I gathered that there was a possibility of reaching *for* freedom, where students and I could engage in conversations, exchange ideas, as well as teach and learn from one other, even in the presence of discomfort, anger, and disagreement. Thus, the student comment, "the hell with English," was a reactionary statement to the quoted text from Taylor. However, it was also an opening from which student voice (e.g., "we actin' like she lyin'"), opinions (e.g., "we can't do nothing to stop them changes"), and examples from lived experiences (e.g., "money coming in my family ain't got") surfaced in the classroom. Not only were we examining a specific context, Harlem, but we were attempting to do what Karimah (from the opening of this chapter) asked: "Be real 'bout things 'cause we know they feed our frustrations." It is this type of feeding of frustrations that I sought to center in class discussions and assignments in order for students (and for me) to "experience breaks" and gain an "awareness of possibility" as we disrupted the normalized patterns, routines, and conversations of school, schooling, and inequitable structures, particularly in this urban context.

Throughout the semester, we revisited the passage from Taylor's book alongside readings written by, among other writers, Paulo Freire (*Pedagogy of the Oppressed*), Jonathon Kozol (*Shame of the Nation*), William Ayers (*City Kids, City Teachers: Reports from the Front Row*), and Langston Hughes ("The Negro Speaks of Rivers"; "The Weary Blues"; "Theme for English B"; "Harlem [2]"; "Lenox Avenue: Midnight"; "Juke Box Love Song"; "Harlem Night"; "I Dream a World"; see Rampersad, 1995). We listened to commentaries on the political and educational directions in which the United States was headed, and we critiqued popular song lyrics, videos, and mass media depictions of urban education (e.g., *Freedom Writers*). Additionally, we debated and sometimes argued over the deeper meanings behind words such as *community*, *power*, *belonging*, *voice*, and *struggle*.

All along, we returned to our collaboratively designed course goals and objectives as we crafted essays, poems, speeches, and multi-genre projects that focused on a number of issues, including responsibility, democracy, loss, and feelings of alienation. Indeed, we successfully fought a lot of battles: rewriting course assignments; negotiating required readings; making space for non-school-sponsored reading/writing activities; mapping ways out of tumultuous friendships and other relationships. We also lost many battles: living up to our huge goal that every student would be on, if not above, grade level before the end of the year; that everyone would stay in, and graduate from, Perennial; and that those experiencing personal loss would seek help from a caring adult (e.g., school counselor, a trusted teacher, family friend) without internalizing

loss in self-destructive ways. Other battles we were confronted with included not engaging in negative confrontations with students (e.g., fighting) and
teachers (e.g., calling them "stupid," sleeping in class), illnesses, hunger issues,
and feelings of frustration with academic underpreparedness.

CASES AND CONDITIONS: LOOKING AHEAD

I am aware that the spaces I take up in this chapter do not resemble actual
cases in the research sense of understanding and conducting "case studies."
Clearly, there are methodological underpinnings of this type of research that
frame "an empirical study" in examinations of events, conditions, and phe-
nomena through the use of multiple data sources (see Barone, 2004; Stake,
2000; Yin, 1984). Yet I do believe that information (e.g., archival data, in-
terviews, observations, fieldnotes, course artifacts, personal reflections) collected about the local context of East Harlem and about Perennial—the high
school and English classroom/course—is information about cases. These cases
reveal many complexities surrounding teaching and learning for possibilities,
openings, freedom, and justice. Whether it is Veronica, the principal, talking
with me about needing to work toward a school-wide culture of equity and
excellence, Victor asking his peers and me to "take stock of commitments
to the school," or Quinton loudly proclaiming that "SCHOOL'S BORING.
WHAT YOOOUUU EXPECT," the various cases represent specific patterns
and conditions that "provoke [us] to break through the limits of the conventional" (Greene, 2000, p. 109). These cases return me to the student-devised
context-specific inquiry questions that I highlighted at the beginning of this
chapter: What do students think of the school? What types of activities and
engagements go on there? Does this school, and what happens at this school,
contribute to students' literacy levels and everyday lives? What could students
do to improve, maintain, and/or build upon both the school environment and
surrounding community space? Are people at the school committed to equity
and diversity, and is this commitment obvious? How can we tell?

It may appear that I implicitly focus on these questions in the following
chapters. In fact, that is a purposeful move. I spend the next three chapters
providing specific examples of students' literacy acts and engagements as I
build toward a more explicit discussion, in the closing chapter, of these acts/
engagements in relation to the aforementioned inquiry questions. This allows
me to first turn attention to students' literacy activities and resistances, given
that they have a lot to say about the contexts of teaching and learning. I
believe it is time for those who care about schooling and the education of
children and young adults to listen with open hearts and open minds. The
students presented in the next chapters represent people who are questioning
context in order to break through and see beyond the surface of things.

CHAPTER 3

Damya's Democracy

Classrooms as Sites of Literacy Engagements

We sat at tables, each table facing the front of the room, which was lined with wall-mounted chalkboards and where an unused teacher's desk, covered with old books and handouts, sat to the left. The tables were divided into two sections so as to have an aisle running down the middle of the classroom. This seating design was imposed on us from our very first class session, and we hesitated to change it because different classes at Perennial occupied this room before and after our English class. For the most part, students self-selected their seating assignments, and on occasion, a few students would periodically reseat themselves based on group work and discussion topics. Students comfortably and regularly brought their conversations—from their other classes, volunteer meetings in the library foyer, or outside of school—with them as they crossed the threshold into our English classroom. But on this day, something was different. Instead of hearing students talk about a headline story from the *Daily News, The New York Post,* or an early morning television or radio show, I heard: "I can't believe some schools like that"; "How kids learn in them environments?"; "What kind of society we live in that don't value education enough to make sure all kids got at least the basics to learn?"; and "Somebody must think that's too much to ask."

With these sentiments, students walked into the classroom in an unusual combination. The first few students walked in one after another, and then groups of two students entered side-by-side, which was followed by small groups of students entering the classroom clustered together. Students who were normally late to class were there either early or on time. Surprisingly (at least to me), as students entered the classroom they moved the tables from their normal forward-facing position and into a distraught-looking, but welcoming circle. Chairs were scattered everywhere. Students tossed their backpacks either on top of the tables or on the floor. With crossed arms or with their hands holding up their cheeks, they stared at me, without a smile or a "Good morning." As I was about to take attendance, Karimah said, "Really, Miss? Where we gonna start?" I tossed the attendance sheet aside, leaned on one of the tables, and commented, "I'm not sure what you're talking 'bout, so why don't we get started with what's on your minds? Who wants to get us going?" Damya jumped in.

GETTING GOING AND SEARCHING FOR ANSWERS

"He got me with his chapter titles: 'Dishonoring the Dead'; 'Hitting Them Hardest When They're Small'; and 'The Ordering Regime.' Those aren't the only ones that stick out like somebody slapped me in the face with a sore thumb." A few people laughed at Damya's extended use of the idiom— "stick out like a sore thumb"—and someone snickered, "Girl, you crazy." To this, Damya said, "No, what's crazy is: 'Deadly Lies,' or 'False Promises,' or even 'Invitations to Resistance.'" She continued: "I started reading what he had to say, and I'll admit that at times I was bored, but at other times, I was like what? This real? This what some students endure when they try to get an education?" At this latter comment, students started chatting with the person next to them until Damya said, "Wait, let me finish. Now, I know conditions are not like this everywhere, but if conditions like this in one school, that's enough to call for positive changes in the whole system, and yes, I said the whole system." Damya paused, as if to gather her thoughts, and when she looked up at me, she shook her head and uttered, "His titles and arguments real, but they infuriate me. I got questions."

Before I could respond to Damya's questions, Juan commented: "The thing that got me from the jump was Pineapple and how he says Pineapple told him one of her teachers would cuss at the kids to calm them down. How that gonna calm down kids, elementary kids at that? We need to start taking action to change things." With this latter comment, students sat there staring at Juan as if to ask him to continue speaking. Based on students' facial reactions, it seemed to me that many, including myself, were wondering who this young man *really* was—a teenager who often sat in class, told jokes, bothered his peers as they tried to complete assignments, asked to go to the restroom every 5 minutes, and related just about every course reading to his love of baseball. This was a side of Juan, an outspoken, passionate, activist-oriented side, that many of us—his peers and some, if not all, of his teachers—rarely witnessed. As we stared at him, Juan remarked: "I'm being honest, jokes aside. That's just the beginning of what I got to say about points from this book." Everyone sat silently in an otherwise loud, action-packed classroom, waiting for Juan.

His face was painted with a look of shock as he realized that his peers gave him, by virtue of their silence, the classroom stage—a location they battled for on a daily basis. Juan took the stage: "We can laugh all we want about these things, but come on, something's wrong with adults who cussin' at kids or smoking in school. Something's wrong with a system that don't value kids more than this." Everyone seemed to agree with Juan, as indicated by head nods and verbal interjections of "Exactly" and "You got that right." More hands and arms than I could count rose into the air. Instead of waiting to be acknowledged, students quickly shouted out their reactions to comments offered by Damya and Juan. Reactions ranged from "Them titles wild, but they 'bout truth"; "Not like we don't know lazy teachers. Just think back"; to "Truth hurts, 'specially when it hits close to home." Other students offered responses about school culture, schooling and its practices, and issues related to teaching and learning in urban districts: "Makes you think nobody cares 'bout urban students"; "I could teach better than some teachers."

All of the aforementioned comments and those that immediately followed stemmed from our class reading of Jonathan Kozol's (2005) book *The Shame of the Nation: The Restoration of Apartheid Schooling in America*. Students were particularly struck by Kozol's descriptions of schools in urban areas that are labeled "failing" and "underperforming" just as much as they were drawn to how Kozol relies on students', teachers', and administrators' narratives of place to offer visual depictions of "here" (low-performing urban schools with a high concentration of students of color) and "over there" (more well-to-do, White-majority schools). While Damya appeared fascinated and disturbed by the chapter titles, titles that reveal harsh learning conditions for students of color from poor and working-class backgrounds, Juan appeared angry with the actions of teachers who fail to recognize learning as "fun, playful, messy." He even used the phrase "punishing tactics to calm down students" as a way to talk about how teachers think that they are tempering students' behaviors when, in fact, they are silencing students altogether. To demonstrate this point, Juan paraphrased a passage from Chapter 1 in *The Shame of the Nation*: "Did anyone read the part where he's talking 'bout kids eating lunch and watching cartoons and the film keeps skipping? The kids get mad 'cause it skips a lot, and some teacher is like . . ." [Juan interrupts his flow of ideas and turns to Kozol's text to read the passage] "threatening the kids with dire punishments if they did not sit in perfect silence while they waited for the next cartoon" (p. 14).

Without thought, Juan—trying to maximize his classroom time at center stage—then turned everyone's attention to a passage on dual educational systems from Kozol's introduction: "What saddens me the most during these times is simply that these children have no knowledge of the other world in which I've lived most of my life and that the children in that other world would have not the slightest notion as to who these children are and will not likely *ever* know them. . . ." (p. 11). After he read the last words, "*ever* know them," Damya tried to interrupt, but Juan wanted to read more, and he did. He asked everyone to flip over a couple of pages, and he continued sharing excerpts from Kozol's text: "I think you need to go into the schools in which the isolation of our children is most extreme, do so repeatedly, and try to make sure that you are allowed time to listen carefully to children"; "I have almost always found that children are a great deal more reliable telling us what exactly goes on in public school than many of the adult experts who develop policies" (p. 13). Juan stopped reading and talked briefly about the need for adults to listen to, acknowledge, and respect students' perspectives on schooling—what students think they, themselves, need to learn; the different ways students actually learn; and the actions, factors, and situations that discourage students from learning or from demonstrating that they are, in fact, learning.

Damya inserted her opinion by restating ideas expressed by Juan on respecting, acknowledging, and validating students' viewpoints, especially students who are subjected to schools, teachers, and learning that, to use Damya's words, "do little to nurture the souls and support the creativity" of students. As she was talking, I quickly surveyed the room and noticed a few students jotting ideas down on paper, and I asked for other voices to join the conversation. Without hesitation and without automatically looking up at me, Daniel responded: "I'm reading this Kozol, listening to y'all, and I'm like, man, do we live in a democracy 'cause if we did, this stuff shouldn't go on. In a true democracy, *people* [his emphasis] would talk up so positive things happen. Nobody would have to go to schools that don't have right resources. We'd have just as much rights as them other students." Karen jumped in, "Just as much? Whatchu mean, just as much? You mean equal rights, I hope. By 'them other students,' you mean rich White students in rich White school districts, or what?"

Daniel's sentiments, and Karen's interrogation of his sentiments, led to the following in-class exchange, which I audio recorded:

> *Karen:* I got you right, or am I wrong?
> *Daniel:* You right. But my point is I'm wondering
>   what democracy means here.
> *Damya:* When you got democracy, you got people working
>   together, living together, and even growing together. We
>   don't all have to agree on everything, but we should respect
>   each other . . . be open to listening to other people.
> *Daniel:* In a democracy, we don't have room
>   for hate or mistreating people.
> *Celina:* What we got in this country ain't democracy. What they say,
>   "of the people, by the people, for the people?" Mm-hmm, right!
> *Stephen:* Girl, you know those just words the majority of people in
>   power don't follow. That's why I agree [with Celina] we don't
>   have democracy. What we got is like [pause] pretend-to-be-
>   democracy, like a we-want-y'all-to-believe-this-a-democracy.
>   This thing we got hurts people who ain't got power . . . people
>   who poor, Black, Brown, and some White people. That's on
>   the real. Maybe this ain't 'bout democracy as a system, but
>   as ideas and values. *[He points his finger for emphasis].*

VK: Do you think this classroom's a democracy or's democratic? Be honest.

Damya: No, 'cause we got limited power and freedom! Then again, maybe, kinda 'cause it's rooted in like . . . ideas on or maybe in . . . democracy. This class can be our mini-democracy 'cause you always got us practicing being democratic and all.

[Students laugh and some shake their heads at Damya's suggestion.]

Jose: How we got a mini-democracy like this class inside a bigger structure that ain't a democracy, like school, and we know this school ain't a democracy? Is democracy a state of mind or is it really something we can live within? If we talkin' 'bout being democratic, that changes the game.

Daniel: Interesting. A classroom in a school a mini-democracy, but the school not one. But now we sayin' democratic. That's Kozol straight up. He said some have an ideal 'bout education that gets in the way of them seeing what's real, like the students, and what is reality, like the conditions students gotta learn in. I'mah need to think about that some more.

Damya: That means you got some classes where teachers see the wrong and work at teaching the right . . . other classes where the wrong is the only thing that get taught. Some classes practice being fair for the people . . . I guess that's democratic. Others don't and remain against people. I see that as undemocratic. You gotta have that working-together, living-together, growing-together combo to have democracy, or at least to have values that point to being democratic. That's what I think for today.

[Bell rings, and everyone leaves]

"YOU'VE GOTTA HAVE . . . THAT COMBO TO HAVE DEMOCRACY": CLASSROOMS AS SITES OF ENGAGEMENT

I found the above exchange powerful for a number of reasons. First, the idea of democracy entered the conversation without any prompting on my behalf. This was not the first time phrases such as "being democratic" and "having democracy" surfaced, as I later discuss in the examples of Damya's literacy artifacts (below). However, Daniel's reading of Kozol's text and his thinking around what it means to live in a democracy in light of educational injustices directed toward students of color moved the class to more deeply consider democracy as connected to schooling. In this connection, students skillfully reframed traditional conversations on democracy as a political system of governance where you have those who rule/those who are ruled to discussions on people taking up/engaging in/doing "positive things" in order for all students and all schools to have the "right resources" (Daniel's comment). To have a more widespread, impactful taking up of positive things (e.g., educational changes, adequately resourced schools, acknowledging the wrong by "teaching the right"), a balance must be present among the ways people work together, live together, and grow together (Damya's suggestion). Otherwise, efforts in sustaining a democracy would result in what Stephen calls "pretend-to-be-democracy . . . [that] hurts people who ain't got power."

Other equally provocative points were raised throughout the exchange: a classroom existing as "a mini-democracy" within a larger institutional structure; teaching as wrong/teaching the wrong (undemocratic) and teaching as right/teaching the right (democratic); and debates on having a democracy and/or being democratic—the latter of which I refer to as Democratic Engagements (see Figure 3.1). While the word *power* was only stated twice by Stephen and once by Damya in the entire exchange, it was implied in the ways students talked about being "open to listening to other people," "being fair for the people," and "remain[ing] against the people." Undoubtedly, the exchange was highly personal and political, and, I argue, grounded in a level of critical consciousness that, according to Nieto and McDonough (2011), "involves critiquing relations of power, questioning one's assumptions about reality, and reflecting on the complexities of multiple identities" (p. 366). While Nieto and McDonough discuss critical consciousness (see also Freire, 1973) in relation to the training of pre-service teachers, I think it is also necessary to think about such consciousness from the perspectives of young people, particularly those attending schools in urban contexts (Ginwright, 2010; Hill, 2009; Kinloch, 2010a; Vasudevan, 2009).

In the remainder of this chapter, I draw on points from the above exchange to think through the idea of Democratic Engagements (Kinloch, 2005) in teaching and learning with students at Perennial. I describe Democratic Engagements (DE) as situated practice to demonstrate how this materialized in classroom discussions and throughout course activities. While some students embraced opportunities to perform (Fishman, Lunsford, McGregor, & Otuteye, 2005) aspects of DE, others grappled with implementing its meanings, tenets, and practices in class work (e.g., in their writings, presentations, in group discussions). As indicated by Rosa, a Latina student in the course: "This a new and strange practice, talkin' upfront 'bout power, really listenin' to people to push my thinkin' cause now we gotta make decisions 'bout school work, like what we gonna write, present, or put on the floor for people to pick a part and try to put back together. Pressure's on." I draw on Rosa's sentiments about the pressures that come with students practicing DE as I present two additional scenarios from the English course. These scenarios center on Damya's literacy artifacts—an essay on Langston Hughes's poem "The Weary Blues" (Rampersad, 1995), and a response and

Figure 3.1. Democratic Engagements

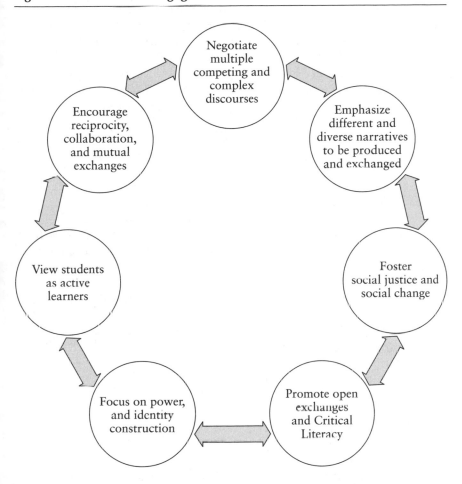

an argumentative writing sample on points from Kozol's (2005) *The Shame of the Nation*. Taken together, Damya's artifacts, and her peers' responses to them, point to the resistances with, and potential around, supporting Democratic Engagements in classrooms.

DEMOCRATIC ENGAGEMENTS AS
SITUATED PRACTICE IN TEACHING AND LEARNING

Kozol's *The Shame of the Nation* stimulated highly charged discussions among students in my English course on teaching, learning, power, and democracy in urban schools. As students talked about selected passages and struggled to make sense of inequitable teaching and learning conditions within the schools described by Kozol, they were participating in Democratic Engagements (Kinloch, 2005). As situated practice, DE is contextualized within the lived conditions, voices, and histories of, as well as interactions among, people within defined communities. That is, as students in the course questioned larger arguments presented by Kozol, and as they engaged in self-reflexive inquiry, they were collaborating on, reaching for, and investigating larger meanings of education in what they initially believed to be a democratic society. Hence, the comments offered by both Celina and Daniel, respectively: "What they say, 'of the people, by the people, for the people?'"; and ". . . Some people have an ideal 'bout education that gets in the way of them seeing what's real . . . and what is reality." Such actions—critical questioning, listening, investigating, responding, and being reflexive—point to practices in Democratic Engagements.

Elsewhere, I argue that DE is grounded in "the ideals of education, the values in literacy acquisition, and the principles of creative pedagogies [that encourage] conversations and relationships people have with one another in multiple spaces of interaction" (Kinloch, 2005, p. 109). DE seeks to bring into alignment two specific domains of practice—schools (and academic conventions) and community (and local practices)—by highlighting the following:

- Learning as contextualized, multiple, and complex
- Learning as collaborative
- Learning as reciprocal
- Learning as rooted in mutual respect
- Learning as knowledge construction
- Learning as active/always becoming
- Learning as engaged participation
- Learning as democratic
- Learning as social justice
- Learning as grounded in multicultural education
- Learning as framed within equity pedagogies

In order for such constructions of learning to exist, it is important for learners to be cognizant of their shifting roles and identities, even as they occupy particular authorial positions (e.g., principal, teacher, researcher, and student government president). Figure 3.2, "Positions of Learners," outlines learning as generated by (as well as among and across) multiple people and as centered in the exchange of knowledge (e.g., information, perspectives, histories, lived conditions, textual evidence). This way of thinking about learning and learners allows DE to flourish in constructive ways.

Establishing explicit connections with *engaging* in learning and *being* democratic provides a framework for teaching and learning that opens up expansive possibilities for students to participate in collaborative meaning-

Figure 3.2. Shifting Positions of Learners Around Learning and Knowledge

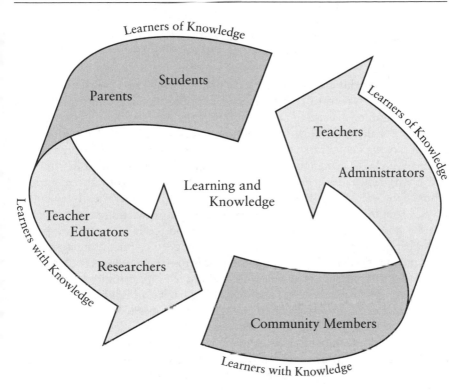

making, text-making, and community-building processes. Torre and Fine (2006) describe this form of participatory learning as having "democracy and justice" at its core (p. 269). Darling-Hammond (1996) calls this type of learning *education as democracy,* because "students [are given] access to social understanding developed by actually participating in a pluralistic community by talking and making decisions with one another and coming to understand multiple perspectives" (p. 6).

In this way, DE speaks to an ideological model of literacy, a model shaped by social contexts (e.g., schools, communities, and other locations) as well as by relations of power. DE in classrooms relies on "the notion of democratic practice," which, according to Schultz (2009), "hinges on re-framing classroom participation as engaged participation whether verbal or silent, through auditory or visual modes" (p. 119). This model is especially important for how I understand learning as multiple (see above) and democracy as a community that is always being shaped/reshaped, framed/reframed in productive ways. Here, I rely on Greene's (2000) definition of democracy:

Democracy, we realize, means a community that is always in the making. Marked by an emerging solidarity, a sharing of certain beliefs, and a dialogue about others, it must remain open to newcomers, those too long thrust aside. This can happen even in the local spaces of classrooms, particularly when students are encouraged to find their voices and their images. (p. 39)

What does this mean for teaching and learning, and for the ways students in my class read Kozol's text as well as other texts? Countless students skillfully adapted aspects of Democratic Engagements in their literacy work. They questioned meanings of schooling as associated with *having* democracy and *being* democratic. Students listened to one another in a supportive, interactive classroom environment, one that was not absent of disruptions and chaos. They read, interpreted, interrupted, and wrote about various school- and self-sponsored texts in collaborative, democratically engaging ways. From investigating themes in course readings, writing poetry that expressed personal understandings on nationhood, collaborating in a group with peers who on the surface did not get along, to re-imagining an assignment prompt through songwriting and guitar playing, students took responsibility for their learning. At times, this taking of responsibility materialized in the form of student silence, acts of talking back and talking against, and moments of outright resistance to engaging in schoolwork.

During these learning moments—moments that reflect ideals of, and struggles with, Democratic Engagements—I sought to do what Greene (2000) suggests: "Affirm and reaffirm the principles that center around belief in justice and freedom and respect for human rights," because, as Greene testifies, "without these, we cannot call for the decency of welcoming and inclusion for everyone, no matter how at risk" (p. 43). Without these actions and principles, we teach and learn in the absence of democracy, in the absence of Democratic Engagements, and in the absence of learning that is, that becomes, framed within equity pedagogies.

DEMOCRATIC ENGAGEMENTS IN PRACTICE

With this working understanding of Democratic Engagements as situated practice, I offer two specific classroom scenarios that speak to learning as collaborative and learning as democratic. In the first scenario, I describe how Damya takes up larger themes from Langston Hughes's "The Weary Blues" through a close reading of, and subsequent writing and presenting on, the poem. The second scenario focuses on a response and an argumentative essay that Damya wrote on ideas from Kozol's *The Shame of the Nation*. In both scenarios, I note the ways she creates what I call a "second text" as she establishes personal connections to "The Weary Blues" (scenario #1) and as she considers ways to speak back to issues around race and segregated schools (scenario #2). A second text is writing that represents one's stream of consciousness, a stream that flows into—but appears disconnected from—one's current writing/thinking/talking about the primary text, an author, or a moment under investigation.

Often, it appears that a second text does not offer supporting evidence for one's understanding of the writing topic or prompt, for its inclusion is often seen as a deviation from the central line of argument being made. Nevertheless, a second text can offer students ways into and then successfully out of required writings by providing opportunities for them to relate what they know (prior knowledge from school or home) to the production of the actual writing assignment. Thus, a second text creates more tangible openings for students to form personal connections with the main topic or prompt. The two scenarios described below point to the value of a second text in students' literacy engagements, which then points to practices in DE.

Damya and Learning as Democratic: For the Love of "The Weary Blues"

Damya is an African American female who walks with a sense of grace and dignity, embodies friendliness and warmth, and has a down-to-earth demeanor. She is a self-identified reader and writer who enjoys composing poetry and prose and is enamored by the use of language in print and oral forms. During a class study of literary writers of color, Damya read numerous poetic selections by Langston Hughes. She was intrigued by his "poetic taste in words," "poetic style," and "irony, personification, and metaphors," as well as by the "figurative language throughout 'The Weary Blues,'" because, according to Damya, "Hughes shows that blues comes from a place of real life inspiration." In her essay titled "Langston Hughes and the Blues," Damya focuses on the poet's use of language in order to paint a picture of a complicated writer and narrator who not only wrote about "singing a blues tune, but expressing what is felt in his soul, which was empty, stranded, and alone." On this latter point, she writes that the figurative language used by Hughes "represents a man, maybe him or maybe not him, who is suffering emotionally and mentally because he feels alone in the world." She continues:

> When he says, "put ma troubles on the shelf," it seems as though he doesn't want to feel this lonely way anymore, so he is relieving himself from those feelings by singing it out to others. This language gives off a feeling of deep blues, as though his blues are not just a tune. . . . In some way . . . this poem reflects what happens when dreams are no longer dreams and visions of rapture are no longer visions of rapture. . . . Black people used blues as a means of expressing their feelings, fears, and beliefs about the world.

Damya's essay continues with descriptions of someone "feeling alone and saddened" who turns to music for comfort. At this point, she engages in an important shift in her thinking and writing about Hughes's "The Weary Blues" (Rampersad, 1995), one that leads to her personal connection to larger themes of identity, struggle, and perseverance. In one instance, she writes in her essay about the blues as weary/as pain that needs to be relieved. In another instance, she creates an additional, or second, text—a poem she wrote—as a way to connect the pain from "The Weary Blues" to a fear of being subjected to an unforgiving world in which she herself was born, but that offers her no protection. The following is an excerpt from Damya's poem (a second text) that she included near the end of her essay. The poem is titled "My Beautiful":

> My Beautiful, beautiful America
> When did you become so corrupt?
> Why did you turn out this way?
> Is it because of man's ideal society?
> Is it because the words American citizen
> Have no meaning any longer?
> Why do you have to close your eyes and ears
> To those who are really in need?

Later in the same poem, Damya questions what it means to belong in a place (America) that does not want you/that rejects you:

> I was born here, but why do I ache?
> Questioning every day.
> Or, saying, just another day of living in America.
> My children have no better future than I do.
> My God, my God, why?
> Why must we live in a world in which cards or
> Little pieces of paper define us?
> Why do I wake up every morning in constant fear of not seeing
> Every single member of my family?
> Was my birth a dream?
> Was my birth not fit for a world such as this?

Throughout her poem, Damya offers descriptive insights into her thinking-questioning processes by referring to her perpetual search for "a better world" in which sisters, brothers, daughters, and other innocent people could retreat. Nevertheless, she admits, much like Langston Hughes does in a number of his poems, that "being an American has its consequences."

Eventually, Damya's poem ends, as does her essay. Skillfully, she makes visible the connection between her writing about Hughes's "The Weary Blues" and the inclusion of her poem "My Beautiful." In doing so, she confesses that she wonders why more people do not speak against pain, wrong, and injustices, a point that brings to my mind Audre Lorde's (1980) plea for people to turn silence into action and language. Damya's essay thus ends:

> I speak when I feel inspired and when I see wrong, and my poem connects to poems by Langston Hughes because his poems are about things that inspired him to write for change. Real life events and realities that he wants people to know; he wants people to understand what he already understands. Hughes' poetry reflects a man, or an author and a narrator, who is gifted and wants to share that gift with people from all ages, races, genders, and generations. He is a legend that will never be forgotten.

During one of our class sessions, Damya stood before everyone, insisting on getting their attention, and she did. Then she offered an overview of her essay and read an excerpt from her poem, her second text. By doing so, she willingly opened up a space for peer feedback that required her to listen to and consider other people's opinions.

The following student exchange, which occurred immediately after Damya's presentation, reflects a view of learning as collaborative, as rooted in mutual respect, as engaged/engaging, and, among other things, as democratic (DE):

Rosa: Girrrrrlll, that was gooooooooddd [her emphasis].
Damya: Thanks. What made it good, though?
Rosa: Your reading of the poem. How you focus on struggle. How you say something like, "the writer or the narrator," like you separating out the two [positions]. Just the respect you show when you write about "Weary." You got me thinking, girl.
Sharif: I read that poem and didn't even think about him internalizing pain like you did. Like the pain from living everyday life and trying to survive, trying to do good. And, and . . . the struggles with wanting to make it. You got me seeing how Langston was writing about how pain can be expressed in song and in body.
Damya: Can I borrow that phrase? I'll give you full credit . . . "How pain can be expressed in song and in body." I like that phrase.
Sharif: Yeah, you can borrow it, but how you gonna use it? I think you should write a poem about it or put it in your essay. You could talk about Black people expressing pains by using song . . . also what we do to our bodies. Our bodies can be weary.

That's his word [Langston Hughes], then again, bodies can be temples that help us deal with life and the pains. Anyway . . .

Damya: I'mah quote you. Maybe you can help me diagram that out.

Sharif: We can do that.

Rosa: That's deep. Y'all bouncing off each other and gonna work together. That's deep.

Michael: I wanna say something. I feel like you should make the tie-in stronger . . . why you including your poem? How that tie to Hughes? You said you wrote the poem way before doing the essay. Can you like reflect on how you feel about your poem now . . . kinda like giving a building up of your ideas and your poem.

Damya: Explain that.

Michael: I mean somehow Langston made you think about the fact that you wrote the poem a while back, and you remembered you wrote it because reading Langston made you think about it. I don't know what the word is for this, but like, you gotta reflect on your thinking . . . explain why you put the poem in the essay. . . . Somebody help me out.

Patricia: Reflect on your choice. Why you did what you did. Ain't that right, Miss [looking at me]? C'mon, Miss, you know that's [pause] DEM-O-CRA-TIC!

[She laughs, which provokes some students to get slightly off topic. Many started chanting DEM-O-CRA-TIC, DEM-O-CRA-TIC, as they forgot that Damya was still presenting. Damya smiled at me, and neither one of us interrupted their DEM-O-CRA-TIC engagements.]

Damya: I see what you mean [*talking to Patricia*]. I like that.

Rosa: Girl, that was good.

Daniel: That's all Rosa gonna say.

A few students laughed at Daniel's closing comment. Damya thanked everyone, returned to her seat, and gave the eye to those who were talking off topic. Sharif came to sit next to Damya and they started talking about "how pain can be expressed in song and in body." Students started chatting about homework from math class. Class ended, but students were slow to leave.

Together, Damya's essay on "The Weary Blues," her poem "My Beautiful," her presentation, and the feedback generated by students reflect aspects of Democratic Engagements that center learning as collaborative, reciprocal, and always becoming. For instance, her close, purposeful reading of, and writing on, "The Weary Blues" afforded Rosa an opportunity to safely name particular strategies taken up by Damya: "The writer or the narrator . . . separating out the two." Additionally, Damya's close textual engagement helped Sharif recognize a specific way of "internalizing pain" in ways where "writing about . . . pain can be expressed in song and in body." As Sharif invited Damya to think about this connection—writing, being weary, and expressions performed through song and in body—Michael offered a related suggestion. He wanted Damya to more explicitly reveal her "building up of . . . ideas" (her thinking process) in order to, in the words of Michael, "reflect on your thinking . . . explain why you put the poem in the essay." The collaborative nature of learning, in this example, became more evident when Michael asked for someone to explain his ideas for the sake of clarity. Without hesitation, Patricia jumped in: "Reflect on your choice. Why you did what you did." In other words, students were pushing Damya in metacognitive ways (e.g., knowing what you know, reflecting on your process of knowing and doing).

Thus, if education is to be democratic, which I argue for, then students' voices, perspectives, readings of the word, and their trying on of different roles (e.g., presenter, listener, respondent to ideas) should be the centerpieces in classrooms. As well, Patricia's DEM-O-CRA-TIC and the ensuing laughter and chanting that followed are also a part of both the process of centering and the construct that education is democratic/education as democratic.

Damya, Democracy, and *The Shame of the Nation*

Nearly 2 months after Damya wrote and presented her essay "Langston Hughes and the Blues," the class read Kozol's *The Shame of the Nation*. As stated previously, students were infuriated with the physical and educative conditions, as described throughout the book, under which students learned. Damya was committed to her idea: "When you got democracy, you got people working together, living together, and even growing together. We don't all have to agree on everything, but we should respect each other . . . at least be open to listening to other people." Her sentiments found their way into her various writings on Kozol's book, especially her responsive essay and argumentative overview journal, as well as in her discussion comments.

During the early stages of class discussion on *The Shame of the Nation*, Damya admitted her hesitations with reading the book. In her journal entry, she wrote: "I just couldn't get into it at first"; "I wasn't sure how he'd use the word 'apartheid' to talk about schools"; and " I get turned off by other people talking about Black and Hispanic kids in predominately (Black/Hispanic) public schools." Other students expressed similar concerns with the book. Rajon, an African American male in the class, took issue with "negative views people got of us, and those people don't even know us. Like we all the same and they experts on us. That rubs me wrong. I hope this Kozol dude don't do that." Rajon and Damya had a way with words, a way that rallied the majority of students in the class to either side with or take issue with their perspectives, and when someone took issue with them, Rajon and/or Damya would comment, "Turn to the text. Tell me where you see that [point]. Hand me evidence." Over time, Damya, as with Rajon, set aside initial hesitations and assumptions with *The Shame* in search of deeper meanings, as indicated by oral and written comments.

In her responsive essay, Damya talks about how she pushed herself "to keep reading and I'm glad I did." She writes:

> I realized the book . . . brings up a lot of hidden topics. . . . His intended topics are real life issues, the reality of public schools, and confidence and environments of Black and Hispanic students. Kozol's intended audiences are everyone, white, black, Hispanic, male, female, congress, board of ed, anyone that wants to know and learn truth . . . about public schools. Kozol's positions on these themes are simple: Does a school carry out its mission? Does the school teach students realities?

From here, Damya makes an interesting move in her writing, one that connects her points—on Kozol's "intended audiences" and "positions on these themes"—with the inclusion of a second text. Unlike the inclusion of her poem "My Beautiful" as a second text in her essay on Langston Hughes's "The Weary Blues," Damya's second text in her responsive essay takes the form of a well-developed yet brief commentary on race and schooling. She begins: "For example, earlier in Chapter 1, Kozol is talking to a girl, Pineapple, who asks him, 'What are the "other people" like?' This shows that exposure of black and Hispanic kids to Caucasian kids is rare in lots of urban schools." Damya turns to Kozol's text to strengthen her argument. She cites passages on segregated schools from 25 to 30 years ago being "no less segregated now, while thousands of other schools that had been integrated either voluntarily or by force of law have since been rapidly resegregating" (p. 18). Damya incorporated into her writing Kozol's passage about the difficulties of convincing "young people that they 'can learn' when they are cordoned off by a society that isn't sure they really can." She agreed with his belief that "this is, I am afraid, one of the most destructive . . . messages a nation could possibly give its children" (p. 37).

These passages, along with her responses to them, served as her second text located within her responsive essay. In this second text, Damya made this point:

> As I now see it, race plays a big part in segregated schooling. Those who are black and Hispanic get the short end of the stick and are less likely to go to schools that have majority white students. I'm gonna change that. I applied to 11 private colleges, all of which are predominately white . . . because I wanna beat the system by taking an up close look inside the system. But anyway, let me get back on point.

By including this second text in her essay, Damya was able to share a personal confession—"I wanna beat the system"—incited by Kozol's references to "other people" and segregated schools. This inclusion also allowed her to reflect on her emerging stance of *being* democratic and employing elements of Democratic Engagements. That is, she utilized practices from school (academic conventions, a responsive essay, persuasive language) and about particular communities (segregation and exclusion, privilege and access, a flawed educational and political system) to assert an active position and offer a direction: "I applied to 11 private colleges." At the same time, she strengthened her essay's argument through inclusion of a second text, which was followed by her concluding thoughts: "I agree with Kozol's argument, does a school board, taxpayer, congress, all of us have no role in what students are suppose to be, how students are suppose to learn?" To think through this question, Damya wrote:

> How are they [students] suppose to learn anything when they go to schools that don't have enough resources or that don't have working lights? Doesn't that send a harsh message to students, come to school to learn, but without appropriate resources! How can anyone say students have a voice, students should be active learners, but do these things without proper resources? Talk about not being democratic.

To more fully demonstrate Damya's leanings toward *being* democratic, I asked students, during another class session, to individually select a passage from Kozol's text. Instead of having students respond to their self-selected passages, I asked them to swap their selections with a student who was not sitting near them. Hector, a Latino student sitting near the back of the room, walked up to Damya and turned her attention to the quite lengthy passage he had selected, which was from Kozol's "Introduction." In its entirety, it read:

> By the end of the 1980s, the high hopes that I had briefly sensed a decade earlier were hard to find. Many of the schools I visited during this period seemed every bit as grim as those I'd seen in Boston in the 1960s, sometimes a good deal worse. I visited a high school in East St. Louis, Illinois, where the lab stations in the science rooms had empty holes where pipes were once attached. A history teacher who befriended me told me of rooms that were so cold in the winter that the students had to wear their coats to class while kids in other classes sweltered in a suffocating heat that could not be turned down. A foul odor filled much of the building because of an overflow of sewage that had forced the city to shut down the school the year before.
>
> I visited, too, the bleak, unhappy schools of Paterson and Camden in New Jersey and similar schools in Washington, D.C., Chicago, San Antonio, and Cincinnati. Back in New England, I spent time with teachers, parents, and

their teenage kids in Bridgeport, where the poverty levels, overcrowded public schools, and health conditions of the children, many of whom had been lead-poisoned in the city's public housing, had created a sense of quiet desperation in the all-black and Hispanic neighborhoods I visited. (p. 7)

In her journal, Damya described the excerpt as "really depressing and sad," given that some students have to attend schools under such horrific conditions. She wrote about taking action and wondered what teachers and administrators were doing to bring attention to these circumstances— "empty holes where pipes were"; "rooms that were so cold"; "classes sweltered in a suffocating heat." In a critical self-reflexive way, she stated, "It makes me appreciate what I have here in East Harlem, although some people might argue that it's just as bad as the school in Paterson and Camden, N.J." Her self-reflexive nature allowed her to make this point: "Being that this was in the 1960s and then 1980s, you'd think some advances would be made toward how the school looks on the inside. But the reality is these schools do not get the real attention that they need to be getting."

A few days after students exchanged passages from Kozol's text, I asked them to pair up with their partners. Damya and Hector sat next to each other, and she asked him what his thoughts were on the passage she selected. The passage reads:

Anxiety, for the children [at an elementary school in the South Bronx], was intensified, according to a fifth grade teacher, by the ever-present danger of humiliation when their reading levels or their scores on state examinations were announced. "There must be penalties for failure," as the architects and advocates of programs such as these [rote-and-drill scripted curricula] increasingly demand, and penalties for children in this instance were dispensed not only individually and privately but also in the view of others, for example in a full assembly of the school. (p. 73)

I saw Hector open his notebook slowly, and he pointed for Damya to read the words on the page. Later, I learned that he wrote 10 words as his journal essay:

I don't like this reality
Devastating
Injustice
Just Wrong
Done!

As I circled the room, listening to various groups talk about their passages, I overheard bits and pieces of Hector's verbal response to Dayma's question: "Why you wrote this?" He explained: "These stories silencing,

man, like paralyzing. I went to a school like that. I got nothing else to say."
From what I could gather, this activity of sharing and responding to excerpts
from the book, at least for Hector, raised past issues around schooling that
he did not want talk about, which in one way may have silenced his voice.

Our many class discussions, group work, and individual presentations
all revealed students who, like Damya and even Hector, struggled to see the
light at the end of the tunnel:

> *Victor:* What kind of society sits back and watch
> students go to unsafe schools?
> *Hector:* Ain't that these schools not safe. They straight
> up dangerous for your health and mind.
> *Jasmine:* How you supposed to learn science . . . by looking down
> empty holes? To sit in a cold class today, a hot class tomorrow?
> *Damya:* Yeah, what kind of society lets this happen?

From the above exchange among Victor, Hector, Jasmine, and Damya,
to the swapping of passages from Kozol's text, to Damya's responsive and
argumentative writings on ideas from *The Shame of the Nation*, concerns
emerged over schooling and its conditions for Black and Latino/a students
in urban districts. Damya's second text on race and schooling, for example,
reveals her thinking about issues of access, power, and change: "I applied
to 11 private colleges . . . because I wanna beat the system by taking an
up close look inside the system." The system that she seeks to beat is one
that has inadequately structured one too many schools for students of color
in urban areas as subpar, or inferior, to schools found in more middle-class
and wealthy White communities. This is a painful realization, one that many
teachers shy away from discussing in classrooms for fear that students would
personalize it. However, I believe it is important to make time and space in
our classrooms for such discussions and investigations to occur. Through the
centering of student collaborations, talk, participatory engagements, writings,
and critical reflections, students can examine such realizations as they question school structures and take up practices in Democratic Engagements. This
way of teaching and learning rejects the restriction of "knowledge production
and learning skills and themes that promote and maintain the status quo," in
order for learning as active/always becoming to not be "negated, submerged,
and dismissed" (Haddix & Rojas, 2011, p. 122).

DAMYA'S DEMOCRACY: NOT YET IMPLICATIONS

As I think about the various lessons I have learned from working at Perennial, watching students debate large sociopolitical issues, and listening to
their language of respect used to communicate tightly held beliefs that are

loosening up at their core, I embrace Ladson-Billings's (1994) observation that "African Americans believed that somehow education could make their dreams a reality. I too believe and hope that if we can dream it we can surely do it" (p. 143). The students in this chapter, from Damya, Daniel, Sharif, Rosa, Michael, Karen, Juan, Stephen, and Celina to the many others, believe in education. However, this belief has been thwarted by the reality of many schools and the practices of schooling afforded to countless students of color in urban districts. Indeed, there is an urgency to dream. As we dream, we must work to improve the teaching and learning conditions for all students, and we must remember not to leave behind the voices, lived conditions, histories, and literacies of the very students who walk into our classrooms.

Undoubtedly, the lessons presented in this chapter, much like the exchanges that are shared in our various classrooms, are specific to the context and the participants. Nevertheless, they are not exclusive to that one context; they are, in many ways, applicable to teaching and learning as democratic in any place, in any classroom, and with any group of learners, so long as they are reshaped to meet the needs, learning goals, and demands of those within specified settings. Whether one chooses to teach selected poems by Langston Hughes, Jonathan Kozol's (2005) *The Shame of the Nation,* Toni Morrison's (1970) *The Bluest Eye,* or any number of canonical, popular, or graphic texts (e.g., graphic novels, manga), one should consider how we—students and teachers—read those texts against the backdrop of learning experiences that are, on the one hand, collaborative, complex, reciprocal, and democratic, and, on the other hand, painful, silencing, and paralyzing.

CHAPTER 4

"Who You Calling a Writer?"

Sincerely,
Robert and Aureliano

Robert directed those five simple, yet powerful words at me—"Who you calling a writer?"—during the very first week of our English class, and when he did, his passion could be felt all across the room. I stared at him, and he back at me. He waited for my reaction, and I waited for his elaboration on not wanting to be called a writer. When neither one of us gave in to the other's stare, Aureliano intervened: "Yeah, who you calling a writer, Miss Valerie . . . *is that what we call you?* . . . I'm not a writer, either. I don't do much on that front." Through his clear voice and out of his sluggish body, one that was topped off with a head full of shoulder-length black hair that sometimes concealed an amazing smile, Aureliano uttered those words, which reaffirmed Robert's resistance to being called and publicly perceived as a writer. There was no pretending that Robert's confession and Aureliano's cosigning of that confession were direct results of an opening comment I made about wanting the class to function as "a community of writers." In this community, I explained, students would write a lot, exchange ideas about writing, and come to a point where they could fully engage in the revision process. Other students chimed in to express their discomfort with my suggestion that we would be such a community, and when I inquired into their levels of resistance, it was Robert who asked: "How many of us see ourselves as writers?" As Damya's and Karen's hands went into the air, Damya responded, "I do." Karen said, "Me, too." Aureliano shook his head from side to side as he uttered, "Well, not the majority of us." Hence, the declaration, "Who you calling a writer?" was pervasive among just about all of the students gathered in the room.

As I reflect on that particular moment—one that included Robert, Aureliano, and their peers' resistance to wearing the label *writers,* and Damya's and Karen's refusal to not be seen as *non-writers*—I cannot help but to think about educational scholarship that has emphasized the historical presence of African Americans as readers and writers (Fox, 2009; McHenry, 2002; McHenry & Heath, 1994). According to McHenry and Heath (1994), "African Americans, through many of the very forms most closely associated with 'oral' features, have based their communication to a great extent on writing and reading" (p. 436). Even with my knowledge of such scholarship and its relevance, I stood there, temporarily frozen, primarily out of dismay, that so many students in this class—African American and Latino/a—outright rejected this label. I quickly assumed that there were layers upon layers of reasons for their resistance. As I gradually dug underneath the surface of things, I learned of their perceptions with, and accompanying tensions around, being positioned as writers, and even readers. It was not that they did not want to be writers; many of them believed they were not equipped with the appropriate skills, schooling, and lived experiences to be, or become, writers.

With these tensions in mind, this chapter interrogates such perceptions of writing and writers held by students in the course. It highlights how Robert, Aureliano, and many of their peers refigured the classroom and course assignments in ways supportive of their lived experiences and untapped academic talents, thus disrupting the idea that they are not writers. To demonstrate their acts of refiguring, I focus almost exclusively on how students re-imagined, or repurposed, required assignments through the employment of nonschool artifacts and texts. In this way, students (re)interpreted classroom work within already familiar examples (e.g., from their own lives, from popular culture, from their local communities) and out of their own personal perspectives. In particular, I present selections of Robert's and Aureliano's writings (e.g., poetry, journal entries) and class projects (e.g., a spoken-word performance, a musical interpretation of an assignment) to demonstrate how they each embodied *writerly stances* even in their resistance to being labeled writers.

To begin, I ground this chapter in a discussion of literature that recognizes the significant role of reading and writing for Black people. Much of the literature referenced here emphasizes important historical perspectives by which Black people acquired literacy, especially during and immediately after slavery, perspectives I rely on as I consider contemporary struggles of Black *and* Latino/a students around reading and writing in school (Ek, Machado-Casas, Sanchez, & Smith, 2011; Martinez-Roldan, 2003). In addition, although there are some studies that focus on adults engaging in writing that "occurs outside formal education" (Gere, 1994, p. 76), I contend that it is equally important to focus on writing by young people that happens within the context of schools. From this brief discussion of relevant literature, I offer examples of course projects completed by Robert, Aureliano, and some of their peers, projects that position students as writers who must come to reject portraits of writers that do not include their histories, images, and diverse communicative forms.

WE ARE WRITERS

Historically, reading and writing for Black people have been associated with the struggle for freedom on both an individual level (e.g., slaves writing their own passes into freedom) and a collective level (e.g., political pamphlets/appeals calling for slave rebellions). Whenever possible, countless enslaved Black people sacrificed their lives—being whipped, raped, hanged, and having fingers amputated—in order to acquire literacy, which "was at the center of the debate about slavery in the 1830s" (Fox, 2009, p. 121). In the face of such obstacles, according to Fox, "African American slaves and freedmen sought literacy as a means of challenging and transforming their communities and the nation. In doing so, they shook the ideological underpinnings of Southern slavery" (p. 122). Such "ideological underpinnings" (e.g., slavery, racism, stolen agricultural labor, brutality, violence, and hatred) came under fire because more and more Black people turned to literacy "to write themselves into being" (Davis & Gates, 1985, p. xxiii). To better understand the extent of people to protect (White people) and acquire (Black people) literacy, one need only turn to Vesey's (1826) plans for rebellion in Charleston, South Carolina, Douglass's (1845/2002) *Narrative of the Life of Frederick Douglass,* Walker's (1969) *Appeal to the Colored Citizen,* and to the onslaught of southern legislation that sought to prohibit slaves from gaining literacy.

In her critique of the philosophy of education of/for African Americans, Perry (2003) asserts the importance of understanding literacy as connected to skills as well as linked to Black people's cultivation of community, mentoring, sense of responsibility, and freedom. She writes:

> While learning to read was an individual achievement, it was fundamentally a communal act. For the slaves, literacy affirmed not only their individual freedom but also the freedom of their people. Becoming literate obliged one to teach others. Learning and teaching were two sides of the same coin, part of the same moment. Literacy was not something you kept for yourself; it was to be passed on to others, to the community. Literacy was something to share. (p. 14)

Perry's assertion parallels Fox's (2009) claim that Black people centered literacy, as both an individual and collective endeavor, in debates against slavery and in pursuit of freedom (see also Holt, 1990; Royster, 2000). This is a noteworthy point, given Anderson's (1988) argument that former slaves valued "literate culture" and sought "to secure schooling for themselves and their children" (p. 5). Clearly, the value of literacy—of learning to write and read, and passing that learning on to others—has played a most significant role in the history of Black people in the United States.

Additional scholarship on Black people as readers and writers has emphasized the emergence of various organizations: the Freedmen's Bureau (Butchart, 1980, 2010; Fox, 2009) during the era of emancipation; Black churches, colleges, and universities, which have been staples in Black communities since antebellum society (Brandt, 2001; DuBois, 1903; Jordan, 2011; Lincoln & Mamiya, 1990; Sias & Moss, 2011); and literary clubs and societies of the Black middle class during and immediately following the turn of the 20th century (McHenry & Heath, 1994). For instance, the Freedmen's Bureau "supervised all relief and educational activities relating to refugees and freedmen, including issuing rations, clothing and medicine . . . [and] assumed custody of confiscated lands or property in the former Confederate States, border states, District of Columbia, and Indian Territory" (The Freedmen's Bureau Online, n.d.). For Fox (2009), the Bureau "concentrated on education at the exclusion of other more urgent political issues (such as land and franchise)." He goes on to state: "As the first system of institutionalized instruction in literacy to African Americans in this country, the Freedmen's schools altered the symbolic—and actual—role that literacy had played in the lives of African Americans" (pp. 123–124).

Even with the existence of the Freedmen's Bureau, it is necessary to account for the history of Black churches in the United States, which reveals their strong influence on the educational, cultural, and political directions of Black people "since their forced arrival to this continent" (Brandt, 2001, p. 111). Brandt writes that one of the many purposes of the Black church was to provide a "tolerated site for congregation, education, and literacy among African Americans, whether enslaved or free" and to engage in "the teaching of literacy and the building and staffing of schools" (p. 111). There is no question that during and after the legalized institution of slavery, many Black people cherished any opportunity by which to acquire and provide others with skills in literacy. Thus, one can make the argument that the Black church, and not the Freedmen's Bureau, was the first established institution—outside of gatherings in homes, at hush-hush harbors, and in secret schools—for the education of Black people in this country.

Black churches were not the only places where Black people valued reading and writing (for research on the literate traditions of Black colleges and universities, see Sias & Moss, 2011). Insofar as the emergence of literary clubs and societies is concerned, McHenry and Heath (1994) describe the literate habits, traditions, and values of Black people dating back to the early 1800s. They ask: "What of those African Americans who chose to write and read in groups in the faith that their writings might help enlighten others—especially the literary reading public? What of those individuals who used their reading of literary works to inspire their own writings and to push their sense of the promise of presenting the life of African Americans through literature? Of those, we hear almost nothing. . . . " (p. 420).

As a way to de-silence the experiences of 19th-century Black middle-class readers and writers who constituted literary clubs and societies, McHenry and Heath called for new ways of seeing literature and literacy outside formal institutional settings (e.g., schools, universities). Doing so, they argue, contributes to a long history of Black people's "orientation toward being literate, aiding in self-improvement, and moving social justice forward with additional 'voice'" (p. 420) that includes, but is not exclusive to, their oral culture (see also Fisher, 2004; Lee, 1992; McHenry, 2002). The role of literacy (e.g., writing/reading), the value of being literate (e.g., readers/writers), and the places that have provided opportunities for literacy (e.g., churches, Historically Black Colleges and Universities [HBCUs], literary clubs, the National Association for the Advancement of Colored People [NAACP], and other associations) represent Black people's commitment to freedom, citizenship, and education.

Thus, when considering the history of reading and writing in the lives of Black people in the United States, it becomes important to juxtapose institutions such as the Freedmen's Bureau, which was primarily, if not exclusively, governed by White ideological perspectives, with the individual and collective efforts of Black people to acquire skills in reading and writing during and after slavery. This juxtaposition reveals the long, complicated struggle of Black people to receive meaningful, high-quality literacy instruction inside and outside of established educational contexts. Furthermore, the resolve of Black people who were committed to literacy during horrific times serves as a powerful counternarrative to current discussions on academic failure and disinterest insofar as the education of Black people, specifically, and people of color, generally, are concerned. "Legitimating these histories in academic classrooms," according to Fox (2009), "has important consequences to teachers and students" (p. 135). This legitimatization becomes crucial in working with students in contemporary public schools who may not readily identify as readers and writers (e.g., Robert, Aureliano), but who come from a lineage of such.

An overview of the history of Black people as readers and writers is important for my critique of students' resistances toward being called writers, at least in the context of an English class in East Harlem's Perennial High School. It proves that Black people have always valued literacy, even in their struggles against organized attempts that sought to prevent them from being literate. I rely on this history—of Black people's pursuit of literacy and the struggles for literacy by other historically disenfranchised people of color (e.g., Latinos/as) in the United States—to examine high school students' perceptions of writing and writers. In this way, I draw attention to writing samples and course projects completed by students who did not readily see themselves as writers, but who came to rely on familiar, personal examples and artifacts by which to write.

ADOPTING A WRITERLY STANCE

In the remainder of this chapter, I present sample writings from, and performances by, Robert, Aureliano, and Rosa. Through presentation of their writings and performances, with attention paid to interpretive strategies and associations with familiar examples, I hope to reveal their *writerly stances* in light of their resistances with being called writers. By *writerly stance*, I refer to what DiPardo, Storms, and Selland (2011) describe as a "sophisticated style to communicate stance or attitude" (p. 17) with a "human presence" (p. 12). In other words, a writerly stance can include the voices, moves, dispositions, and attitudes of students who engage in meaningful writing activities. A major implication of seeing Robert, Aureliano, and their peers as writers who embody writerly stances, as I describe near the end of this chapter, includes teachers' willingness to create space in the classroom for students "to assert their agency and their humanity" (Fairbanks & Price-Dennis, 2011, p. 144).

How Fast Can You Run?
Aureliano and Rosa as Writers Performing Writing

We had only 15 minutes left before class ended, and both Rosa and Aureliano needed to present their projects. "Are you up for it?" I asked them. Rosa shook her head and whispered a soft "Yes," and Aureliano replied, "If you ready. Can we make it?" I nodded, and he stood up. Then, I asked students to follow Aureliano. We left everything—books, bags, and jackets—in the classroom and ran down the hall to the music room for the last presentation of the day. The music room was quite spacious and seemed to be home to just about every musical instrument imaginable. I was somewhat surprised by this, given that many public high schools in New York City no longer have a music room, let alone a music program. This was truly a gem.

When we arrived, students who were in the middle of their class greeted us at the door, and Mr. Ryan, the music teacher, invited us in. Everyone found a seat, leaned against the wall, or squatted in a seating position. There was neither an empty chair available nor an inch of floor space visible. Students—those in my English course and in Mr. Ryan's music class—looked as if they had no idea what was about to unfold in front of them. Rosa went up to the microphone, Aureliano to the guitar, and Mr. Ryan to the keyboards. Once they ran through what seemed to be a 30-second warm-up, the presentation officially began. Rosa introduced it by reading the following from an index card: "We've talked of how writers write and different things, like steps or processes used. Today, I'm sharing a different kind of writing. . . . Miss [Valerie] says it's composing. I say it's writing. You tell me." She then started to sing—three original songs all about a combination of themes: love, abandonment, and searching for an identity in a world, according to

Rosa, that "don't want to accept you like you are." Before each song, she offered a brief overview of her connection to it. For song number one, on love, she read from her index card: "We all want to be loved. I want parents and friends to love me. Even when it looks like the world is crashing in." For the second song, on abandonment, she referenced a spoken-word poem our class had studied a few weeks prior by Jessica Care Moore (1997) titled "Keisha and Other Girls Who Dream with Their Eyes Open." Instead of explaining the poem's connection to her selected theme of abandonment, Rosa read a few lines from it: "There is a mark in the path/connecting reality with our souls/And I'll die there when I run out of poems" and "Smiling at the possibility of looking happy/Despite the cuts I got on my knuckles/From beating myself down." Finally, when Rosa reached her third song, on searching for an identity, she explained, "I think the first two songs come together to make this one."

Once she was finished talking and singing, students in the audience clapped, cheered, and whistled, reactions that Rosa later told me she had never received "in life." Her peers were so supportive that they stayed in the classroom until the performance was over and their questions, directed at both Rosa and Aureliano, were asked and answered: "What motivated this?" "Were those original songs, or poetry to music?" "Do you see poetry and music as the same?" "How you come up with this . . . interpreting themes from readings through music?" "Did anyone else know she sings and he could play like that?" Everyone in the music room that day was late to their next period, and I did not mind writing notes or walking students to their classrooms after they retrieved their personal belongings that they left behind in our classroom. Once everyone was gone, I found a corner in the school and wrote the following fieldnotes:

> Rosa presented her project today. She has a beautiful voice, soft and soulful, in such a tiny body. She was awesome, and Aureliano just fantastic. It was great to see Aureliano stepping it up . . . encouraging Rosa to sing. He whispered, he told her "close your eyes, feel the words." When she did, he closed his eyes and played that guitar like there was no tomorrow. Aureliano? Aureliano? Aureliano, the guy who sits in class, doesn't show me a one piece of writing, and claims to not like writing or anything close to it. Amazing.

There was not enough time for Aureliano to fully present his project; however, his project was directly tied into Rosa's project. She sang and he played the guitar. In collaborating on the performance, they had agreed on the three themes—love, abandonment, and identity—and it was Aureliano who took the lead in writing the lyrics to the songs. When I asked for copies of the lyrics, he informed me that he would "clean 'em up" and give them to me by the end of the school week. This never happened, and I am pretty sure that it did not happen because Aureliano was not a fan of turning in written work for feedback or evaluative purposes. Just as much as I was ecstatic about his guitar performance, I was equally disappointed that he did not give me the written lyrics and his explanation of them. It was clear that Aureliano marveled at the chance to perform writing, literally, but shunned requests to submit writing as part of course requirements. Indeed, his actions, much like Robert's, reflected a deep level of resistance to being asked to do and submit written products. Hence, "Who you calling a writer?" became Aureliano's mantra.

After each presentation/performance, students were required to write a brief reflection that indicated their feelings about the presentation; the larger ideas around composing, writing, and identity that surfaced; and any lingering questions that formed. When students arrived at the next day's class session, they could not stop talking about the performance in the music room by Rosa and Aureliano. They were excited by the opportunity to reflect on the experience. Since Aureliano did not have a chance to talk about his involvement in the presentation because we ran out of class time, I offered him the floor. He came forward and read the following reflection:

> How does music and writing relate to poetry? How can ~~you use it to~~ it be poetic? Music relates to poetry because you use feelings and you describe your thoughts music wise. When you write music, you start off with a rhythm. Poetry can also start off with a rhythm, and the rhythm is the heartbeat. ~~The heartbeat gives music and poetry the~~ Music describes who you are. How you are. How you express feelings. How you put your soul into it (the music and poetry). How you take your time to create the rhythm and to let it feel you. It becomes your soul. It becomes you. [strikethroughs by Aureliano]

When Jose asked, "You write music and poetry?," Aureliano responded, "Yes, more music lyrics." When I asked, "So you a writer, right?," he responded, "Absolutely not. Can I sit down?" Although Aureliano retreated to his seat in the back of the room, questions continued to flow from students to him. Victor wanted to know Aureliano's thoughts on music as a tool in self-expression. Daniel inquired into the processes used by Aureliano to write music: "Do you write out the words or do you draw [Aureliano is a very visual person], or write music notes?" Rajon added, "I like the heartbeat," before telling everyone Aureliano and Rosa should become an official, traveling musical duo. Everyone laughed, but agreed.

At the end of class, Aureliano walked up to me and explained that he is a writer, but not the kind of writer I want him to be: "I write music. Create the idea in the body, let it play out. That's not *writing* like you thinking." I just looked at him, and he offered up an awkward grin before saying: "You waiting for my reflection. It's marked up, but here." I was surprised he gave it to me, given that I had to pull teeth to get Aureliano to hand over any of his writings. Before I could thank him, he bolted out of the room. Rosa and Trina were waiting for him in the hallway, and I caught a smile spreading across Trina's face as he walked in their direction.

Aureliano writes lyrics, sees a connection between music and poetry, and understands that the rhythm is the heartbeat. Why, then, does it appear nearly impossible for him to claim a writerly stance, or at the least, aspects of a writerly stance, especially when he already embodies one?

"You Didn't Tell Me You Were Writing That, Aureliano!"

"Dr. Kinloch, I saw Aureliano yesterday writing his little heart away," began Ms. Veronica Owens, the principal of Perennial High School, as I walked into her office. She stood from her chair and walked up to me to say that Aureliano stayed at school until close to 7:00 PM working on an assignment for my class. "He was typing poems," she shared. The following is an excerpt from my field-notes that documents my exchange with Veronica and then with Aureliano:

> Veronica seemed so excited to let me know Aureliano stayed at the school to do his work. She believes he's finding himself more and more, and that's important. As she said this, I noticed a huge smile on her face, but I refused to offer up one in return because I didn't want to appear to be the reason behind Aureliano's decision to stay and work. He was behind it. He stayed at school. He completed class work. He should be given the credit. Veronica said Aureliano likes having discussions and debates, and is getting used to all the presentations they have to do. I wasn't expecting for her to have copies of his poems, but she did and she showed them to me. I took a peek, but wanted to see if Aureliano would give them to me himself. I left the office and headed to class. Aureliano was already there, and early. Our conversation went something like this: "I see somebody turned in poems to Ms. Owens, but my hands are itching for them. I tell you" (Me). "If you'd wait, you'd see I have copies for you" (Aureliano). "My bad. Just wondering" (Me). "See there. I got 'em for you. Don't fall over 'cause you shocked" (Aureliano). We both laughed. Others walked into the class, and we got started.

Although Aureliano reluctantly shared his poems with me, it was apparent that he still grappled with his writerly stance. As is evident in his poem "Untitled," Aureliano knows how to convey voice and how to include a human element and personal edge in his writing.

"Untitled"

Why waste my time
Looking
At the one I love
Looking
To not be looked upon in return.

When I asked him to talk about the underlying meaning of his poem, Aureliano quickly reminded me that we had read Pat Mora's (1986b) "First Love." In that poem, Mora writes of "brown eyes," "gold butterflies," being watched, and doing the "watching." In "Untitled," Aureliano was able to create an image of love that was different from Mora's version in that it did not include being watched by "the one I love" (Aureliano's words). He admitted that after reading Mora's poem, he sought to respond to it by describing a first love that neither reciprocated affection nor "paid you any mind cause they gave you nothing to hold on to." I was excited by how he connected, in contrastive ways, his "Untitled" to Mora's "First Love."

Before I could offer feedback, he drew attention to his second poem, "Black Valentine." He told me he read Mora's (1986a) "Border Town: 1938," and was moved by her focus on borders. She inspired him to "take on another kind of border" (Aureliano's words). I asked Aureliano to read "Black Valentine" to the class to receive their feedback. At this point, students were working in peer writing groups—they were to bring in a draft of a current piece of writing that they had already submitted for a grade or that they were currently working on completing. In small groups, they described their writings to one another by highlighting the argument, purpose, evidence, and counternarratives, and by exchanging suggestions for revision. The purpose of this peer exchange was for students to closely and intentionally focus on one writing sample they felt connected to and wanted to enhance based on suggestions from peers. Each group was responsible for: 1) talking about their writing; 2) creating a visual—a diagram, a map, etc.—that represented themes from their writings; and 3) reporting on aspects of their conversations with the class in ways that highlighted specific writing and revising goals.

I interrupted group work and asked if anyone would object to having Aureliano read to the class one of his poems. Everyone welcomed this interruption for various reasons: "Let's hear what someone wrote." "I need a break from looking at my crappy writing." Aureliano prepared to read "Black Valentine," but from the chair in which he was comfortably sitting. He sat up and then leaned forward as his hair dangled down the side of his face. Whatever he needed to do to divert attention away from him, he would do. "This is 'Black Valentine.'" He continued:

Oh, Black Valentine,
This day
Is the loneliest of my life.
It builds up sorrow and pain.
It started by a stab from a knife
Which drives any mind insane.
Caused by betray,
This made my life,
Any life,
One of misery.
I can't stand the lies,
Worse than all the birds singing
When they cry.
Why can't all these people
Stop pretending?
My world is sad, my world is ending.
This is my valentine, how I started.
This is my valentine, every one is cold hearted.

When Aureliano finished his reading of "Black Valentine," he did not immediately look up, but he did ask, "Any thoughts?" Jasmine was the first to say, "That boy don't think he a writer." To this, Aureliano chimed in, "I'm not. Putting words on paper don't make me a writer." Jasmine was not willing to relinquish her belief: "Tell me what makes a person a writer?"

Aureliano explained that a writer is someone who can do what Pat Mora, Langston Hughes, and Pablo Neruda can do: "Throw words together and have something happen where people look for more." I asked him to talk about a writer's stance, that is, what a writer does, or embodies, in order to "throw words together" as people search "for more." Unfortunately, class time was just about up, and instead of trying to explain the idea of a writer's stance, Aureliano said, "Maybe next time." Little did he know that "next time" was not too far away.

The very next day, I asked students to return to where we had left off the day before: talking about a writer's stance. For the first time since the class had begun, Aureliano's hand went into the air, and after I acknowledged it, he replied: "I thought about it last night and wrote some ideas." He pulled out a piece of paper and read a poem he wrote titled, "green fire kills."

I see the green fire within his eyes.
I see the wrong doing within their lies.
Their unhappiness brings out sorrow.
Sometimes there is no tomorrow.
The blood rushes within his veins.

Causing confusion and bringing him pain.
Life flashes by the hour.
Love blinds with all its power.

Green fire kills,
    it takes away all of your pride.
Green fire kills,
    it destroys everything inside.
Green fire kills,
    the light that blinds you.
Green fire kills,
    all the thoughts in your mind.

Aureliano talked about wanting to share "green fire kills" with the class because when he reads it aloud, it convinces him that he is not a writer: "My rhyming's forced, not consistent," there is not "enough details," and "who in here [classroom] know what I'm writing on?" Because of these things, Aureliano explained, "I'm not a writer. I put words on paper." In terms of a writerly stance, he said he doesn't have one: "I write, not like a writer. You wanna know my stance? I gotta voice like you. I write when I'm alone, depressed. If that's my stance, fine. Doubt it."

Jasmine commented: "You take no credit. Why you afraid to be called a writer?" To everyone's surprise, Christina admitted, "Wish I was half good. Some of y'all, I don't like cause y'all got no reason to act dumb and bad, but y'all do. Like you [Aureliano]." Damya stared at Christina, as if her eyes were saying, "hush." Christina "cut" (rolled) her eyes and turned away. Damya asserted her position on having a stance: "I'm a writer. I use words to express emotions. There's nothing wrong with being a writer, knowing you have a voice and a presence. Sometimes you might write at the drop of a dime, other times you struggle for the right mood."

Students continued to debate what it means to have a writer's stance, or a writerly stance. Just as much as they were trying to convince Aureliano that he is a writer with a clear stance, Aureliano was trying to convince them that he is not one. I agreed with Damya's assessment (stated above), and when I did, Robert burst out with: "When you gonna accept we don't do that? We not writers! We ain't." This was one debate that was far from over.

Robert's Rules: Says Who?

"We not writers" has stayed with me from the very first time Robert echoed those words until now. How could he be so passionate in his rejection that he and his peers are not writers? Was this a tactic by which to defeat my attempts to alter their perceptions about writing and writers? If so, I wasn't falling for it. I know the history of Black and Brown people as readers and writers in the United States, from the times of slavery to emancipation, and in churches, secret schools, literary clubs, and freedom schools. There was no way I would let Robert, Aureliano, and their peers off the hook so easily.

For one of our class sessions, I distributed photocopies of selected passages from *The Autobiography of Malcolm X, As Told to Alex Haley* (1965/1992). Although we were not examining Malcolm X, the civil rights movement, or even autobiographies, per se, I felt it necessary to have students explore ideas on reading and writing by Malcolm X, given the many references students made to "power," "pride," and "identity." As I assumed, everyone had something to say about the excerpts, and Robert was not an exception. I read aloud the following passage:

> I became increasingly frustrated at not being able to express what I wanted to convey in letters that I wrote. . . . In the street, I had been the most articulate hustler out there—I had commanded attention when I said something. But now, trying to write simple English, I not only wasn't articulate, I wasn't even functional. How would I sound writing in slang, the way I would *say* it, something such as "Look, daddy, let me pull your coat about a cat, Elijah Muhammad—" (p. 186)

Robert grabbed onto the line, "In the street, I had been the most articulate hustler out there," and admitted: "I'm not a hustler, but I am an articulate lyricist." This admission was a major opening, one that I had waited for time and time again. Robert confessing to being a lyricist, "an articulate lyricist," to use his words, and to "appreciating Mr. Malcolm's honesty. He had street smarts first." I asked Robert to tell us what he meant by "an articulate lyricist." He responded: "You know Rakim or KRS-One? Those dudes' lyricists . . . lyrical scribes. They don't throw out yo momma jokes. They step out hard to let you know truth."

I was well aware of Robert's references—Rakim and KRS-One—and I agreed with his description of "an articulate lyricist" as someone who tells truth through delivery of powerful messages. However, I wanted more, so I pushed: "What about you, Robert. Whatcha mean you an articulate lyricist?" He came back hard: "Miss Valerie, you ain't even need to ask me that. You seen my writing . . . how I paint a picture of the scene. You heard me spittin' [rhyming, rapping] the other day. I got skills like them dudes who come before me."

Was this not an example of someone claiming a writerly stance—"you seen my writing"; "I paint a picture"; "spittin' the other day"—even in light of his previous rejections toward being a writer and doing writing? Was this not Robert's description of a writerly stance, one that incorporated passion, voice, and a human presence? Before I could push Robert even further,

Abana shook one arm and hand in the air and asked to read the next passage. I said "Yes," knowing full well I was not done interrogating Robert over perceptions of writers and writing.

Abana read the following passage from *The Autobiography:*

> I saw that the best thing I could do was get a hold of a dictionary—to study, to learn some words. I was lucky enough to reason also that I should try to improve my penmanship. It was sad. I couldn't even write in a straight line. It was both ideas together that moved me to request a dictionary along with some tablets and pencils from the Norfolk Prison Colony school. (p. 187)

Because they were sitting right next to each other sharing intriguing looks and small talk, I could not decipher whether it was Celina or Patricia who said: "A dictionary? That's dedication." In my fieldnotes, I noted that some students were nodding their heads up and down or left to right, as others were offering up verbal cues: "That's deep," "Mm-hmm," and "Fo' real!" Most students indicated that they had read parts of *The Autobiography* before and had seen Spike Lee's movie adaptation of it. Still, they remained intrigued by Malcolm X's tenacity, or as Abana named it, "He's ferocious, reading and writing from a dictionary. Who does that?" Aureliano inserted: "A man desperate," and Patricia said, "Homemade education times ten. You can't get that in no school."

I tried to stress the point that Malcolm X was, among other things, a reader and a writer, and that he did not allow himself to be defeated by circumstance— by going to prison and by not getting a school-based education. Robert concluded this discussion by saying: "He didn't fall victim to street life. He knew what he had to do when he got locked up." Robert highlighted the phrases, "get a hold of a dictionary," "not being able to express what I wanted," and "I wasn't even functional." He ended with, "That's what I'm talking 'bout."

Time was up. Class ended.

"Who You Calling a Writer?" Revisited

Robert came up to me a few class sessions later and said: "I'm still thinking about Mr. Malcolm X and his reading and writing." I looked at him and replied: "Go 'head." I could tell Robert wanted to say more; he had a serious look of curiosity on his face. "Last night, I wrote this. . . . " He shoved a piece of paper my way and asked me to read it. Students began to get loud, probably because Christina's antics (see Chapter 5) were wearing thin on them or because they were stressing about an upcoming project. Robert reached for the paper as if to take it back. "Oh, no you don't. Too late." I quickly glanced at Robert's writing and handed it back to him without uttering a word. He knew my reaction was indicative of my desire for him to read his writings to the entire class.

A short while later, Robert got everyone's attention and asked if they were okay with him reading his response on writing and his free-write on love. When they did not object, Robert began reading:

> Writing is collected and documented data, ready for interpretation. Writing is the assembly of thoughts and ideas in a form that can be read or heard and that can get a reaction or cause an argument. [His free-write] Love is an emotion consisting of unconditional bonding. Love is a connection between two things or people that is stronger than anything else. Love is a difficult emotion to understand because it is something that is often misunderstood by many. At this point, my knowledge of love runs short because I don't really understand it myself.

Karimah was the first to respond: "Why you getting all emotional, Mr. Hip-Hop? He in love." Robert retorted, "I ain't in love, just playing around with form: I wanted to do a free-write about something I don't normally think about. . . . I also wrote on hip-hop." To this latter comment, everyone laughed. Karimah bobbed her head as if she knew Robert had with him an original piece on hip-hop.

"This disconnected," shared Robert, "but I'ma read this . . . on hip-hop in the classroom, if y'all don't mind." Although Robert did not share this writing sample with me, I was anxious to hear it:

> One way hip-hop can be taught in the classroom is if one is looking past their interpretations of some of the actual lyrics to get a deeper meaning. Hip-hop can prove to be a valuable source in regards to strengthening the student-teacher relationship. If a teacher listened to the same music as students, I believe that teacher would put together a correlation between the beliefs and views of a student, and the thoughts portrayed in the song. Once this link is in place, it is slightly easier to realize what the students need to work on with schoolwork. In regards to the mindset and the development of the students' social etiquette and habits in school, if a student believes a teacher is not just there to discipline them, but to learn from them, students will check themselves and show more respect to teachers and their authoritarian positions. This can lead to a healthy student-teacher relationship because students will want to learn.

Robert placed so much energy and enthusiasm in his reading of the aforementioned paragraph that it sounded as if he were combining singing and rapping, not simply reading, to convey his message. A few students remarked: "Who wrote that?" and "You copied that from somebody?" It was Damya who looked at Robert and said, "Deep," before turning to the rest

of her classmates and saying, "Next time someone reading, y'all be quiet."
To prevent any potential arguments from surfacing, I jumped in with: "Talk
about it, Robert. Give us a reflection."

He explained that he had been thinking a lot about his level of reading
and writing since we examined excerpts from *The Autobiography*. In so doing, he was beginning to recognize the various forms of writing, or genres,
that he relies on to express ideas: "Sometimes it's a line here and there.
Other times, a poem, paragraph, essay, but mostly rap or hip-hop." For the
next few minutes, Robert basked in his newfound success as a wordsmith, a
term he used to describe his lyrical abilities and word choice, but he refused
my compliment, "You're a strong writer," which was one attribute of a
wordsmith. I wasn't surprised by his refusal.

A few more class sessions had lapsed before Robert returned to excerpts from *The Autobiography*. I remember it like it was yesterday. Robert was hunched over his notebook, Christina was flirting with Stephen
(see Chapter 5), and Damya and Abana were talking about their digital
community project (everyone was required to digitally document aspects
of their community, complete a related writing assignment, and spon-
sor a class presentation on it). During the last 7 to 10 minutes of every
class session, I tried to provide time for "talk back"—for students to
raise questions, ideas, or suggestions related to course readings, writings,
projects, and discussions. This was not always possible to do in a class
that met for less than 50 minutes a day. Most times our "talk back" was
squeezed into the last 3 minutes of class. Yet on this day, Robert inquired:
"Any talking?" Although I had not planned for it and we were behind
schedule, I welcomed it: "Sure."

Robert, Aureliano, Rajon, and Mariana were sitting near each other,
and Robert said: "I'm not trying to start nothing, but do you think there's
a connection between Mr. Malcolm X and today? Like hip-hop culture?"
I wondered where this was going, so I asked for elaboration. Robert, conscious of the audio recorder sitting near him, said he was not trying to
conflate Malcolm X into hip-hop, or vice versa, but he did note what he
considers to be similarities:

> Mr. Malcolm X looked at his situation after going to prison, and
> realized he needed to do something to change it. He was in a physical
> prison and decided to re-evaluate his life. He turned to education to
> figuring a way to read and write. A lot of us might not be in a physical
> prison, but stuck in a mental one and don't see no escape. Sometimes
> all you can do is let your frustrations out through rap and hip-hop.
> Mr. Malcolm X took hold of his situation. He learned to read and
> write. Some of us make sense of situations through music, rapping and
> rhyming and all that's not conniving.

It was obvious that Robert was grappling with larger issues beyond those presented in the excerpts from *The Autobiography* or those found in hip-hop and rap music. In my opinion, he was contemplating his own life—choices, decisions, and "prisons." He gravitated to points from *The Autobiography* as a way to hold tight to his conviction that people do not have to succumb to the bad or the wrong around them, but can rise above particular situations in order to not get "stuck in a mental one [prison]." Although the above passage represented Robert's powerful oratorical skills—he spoke with emotions, aroused emotions in his peers and in me, and knew when to use inflection—it also represented the depth of his ideas and the search for connections across two seemingly opposing moments (e.g., Malcolm X and his self-teachings; hip-hop culture and "rapping and rhyming").

And like our previous classes, time did not allow us the luxury to take up Robert's ideas. The period ended, but not before Damya said, "When you gonna spit?" Robert looked at me, and I said, "Tomorrow, right, Robert?" He just looked at me and walked out of the room.

Tomorrow did come. Class started with Robert discussing his project, a spoken-word-hip-hop-lyrical-sample that he titled "Re-Imagine *Imagine*." His project focused on a popular song titled "Imagine," by rapper Snoop Dogg. As he explained in his reflective essay, Robert "chose the song because it reflects a lot of people in our communities. The song is about how rap and hip-hop changed lives. I believe hip-hop can be a gift for many young people struggling with understanding their current situations." Robert talked about how Snoop's song challenges listeners to try to imagine music and life for Black people without the contributions of rap and hip-hop artists such as "Russell Simmons, Dr. Dre, Easy-E, Biggie, Tupac, and other heavyweights" (Robert, reflective essay). To emulate the verbal artistry of such "heavyweights," Robert shared his piece "Re-Imagine *Imagine*" with the class. According to Damya, "he 'bout to spit." Below is Robert's piece:

"Re-Imagine *Imagine*"

Take a look in my life
Does this jumble make sense?
Imagine the 21st century with hip-hop having no hits.
Can you picture a life without either—the jumble and no hits—
And having someone come in for a takeover?
. . .
How many CD's have you heard while drinking a grape soda?
How many hours spent arguing over who the next Hova?
See me, I'm a 17-year-old black male
Tell me there's no more hip-hop and that becomes

Synonymous to having no more black males
Even though I heard hundreds of songs
Promoting crack sells
Hip-hop really showed me how to tip my hat well
U see, hip-hop never changed
Ever since my daddy listened
See, back then it was rope chains
Now, it's how our diamonds glisten
They still rappin about how much white they pitching
The most absurd thing is all the youth that listen
At 3, a child recognize his favorite playa
U know that diamond encrusted smooth talker
Who seems to make all the paper
Ask that same child who is lord and savior
He's gonna answer "I don't know, stop acting like a hater"
Even though it has its faults, hip-hop reigns supreme in my world
On the same song, u hear "black power" mixed
    with "I'ma be stealin ya girl"

The old timers say that's the devil's sweet words of salvation
To brag about theft, murder, and ya enemy's seduction

You see, after I eat grandma's luncheon
I turn on the music and she wailing, saying cut out that damn cussin
U see, hip-hop is in my thought, my talk, and my walk
You can tell by my delivery, I'm influenced by New York
It's funny how many people listen to this music and then wind up in court
Despite it all, tell me there is no hip-hop,
U might as well stab me in the heart.

SINCERELY,
ROBERT AND AURELIANO

What might Aureliano, Rosa, Robert, and their peers teach us about writing, writerly stances, and diverse modes of communication (e.g., singing, guitar playing, critical self-reflection, spoken-word performances and writings, talk back sessions)? How might teachers and teacher educators create openings in their classrooms and pedagogical practices for students to experiment with form, function, and purpose insofar as writing and writerly stances are concerned? What makes a student a writer, and what makes a student believe that he/she is or is not a writer? In what ways can teachers and teacher educators draw on the history of Black and Brown people as writers and readers in ways that inform our critical engagements with students and because of students? In doing this work, what would it take for teachers and teacher educators to have the courage to insist that students reject images of writers and readers that do not include their very own images?

In this chapter, I have presented various examples that showcase students as writers, or students performing writing, even in light of their resistances with being called writers. One of the possible weaknesses of this chapter is my implicit focus on *how* students refigured the classroom and course assignments in ways supportive of their lived experiences and untapped academic talents. While I may have been less explicit about *how* they did the refiguring and how we negotiated the curriculum, I do believe the examples demonstrate *what* they did: relied on familiar examples (e.g., musical talents, non-school-sanctioned writings, lived experiences), reinterpreted course work, requested "talk back" time, led the class down the hallway and into the music room, demanded that students respect one another especially during presentations, and demonstrated writerly stances. Together, these things point to students disrupting, however unwillingly and reluctantly, the idea that they are not writers.

It is important to invite students to experiment with assignments, to employ personal artifacts and frames of reference in their writing, and to talk about their ideas in the presence of their peers. As the previous chapter on "Damya's Democracy" explored student resistances around Democratic Engagements in teaching and learning, this chapter examined resistances around writing and being labeled writers. In the next chapter, "Cryin' for Christina," I critique similar ideas by drawing attention to the presence of a culture of power in schools and its impact on students' academic preparation and feelings of alienation and miscommunication.

CHAPTER 5

Cryin' for Christina

"Good mornin', Mizz. You look cute today" were Christina's first words to me as she walked into the classroom on this particular Monday morning. As Christina greeted me, her head remained lowered toward the floor, allowing us not to lock eyes with each other. Whenever she assumed this bodily position—lowered head, pursed lips, hands tightly grasping her books—I knew something more was about to happen, something that extended beyond a simple, yet kind "Good mornin'." I was never sure what would come next. So, on this occasion, I responded, "Hi Christina. How you?," as if to interrupt her next move.

Christina was an Afro-Jamaican student of slender build—under 95 pounds—and petite height—no taller than 4 feet 5. Whenever she spoke in class, after wildly waving her arms in the air for acknowledgment or during her many untimely outbursts, she would speak at a rapid pace and dare anyone to ask her to repeat herself: "Y'all betta listen cause I'mah say this once and only once." She knew exactly what to say in order to get under other people's skin and to incite off-the-topic arguments about people in the class and school, about themes from the readings, and about her own love life. Take the following as an example (from my audio notebook):

> *Christina:* Y'all know my man be cute. Don't be jealous.
> *Aureliano:* What that gotta do with the readings, girl?
> *Christina:* The readings 'bout identity? [Everyone stares, waiting for her rationale.] Okay, then. I'm identifyin' y'all jealous "b's" [she says "b's" instead of using the profane word with which she's referring]. Sorry to offend you, Mizz, but I calls it like I sees it. Identifyin' my man: cute. Identifyin' y'all girls: jealous b's [she makes a buzzing sound, as if to sound like a bee].
> *Jennifer:* Christina, back on topic, pleeeaasssee!
> *Christina:* On topic . . . y'all jealous of my love life and me being cute, right, Stephen [her "boyfriend"]?

Stephen did not respond to Christina. In fact, he did not even look in her direction. Everyone, for the most part, tried to "talk back" (Kinloch, 2009) to her, and as they did, voices grew in quantity. Voices became louder and louder, and tempers began to flare. Christina managed to turn class reading discussion into a focus on herself, something she attempted to do regularly. At times she succeeded. At other times she didn't. This was one of the times when she succeeded. Another time she succeeded was on that Monday when Christina entered the classroom with a lowered head. Something was definitely brewing.

On the particular Monday morning in question, Christina walked in, greeted me, dropped her books off atop the table where she was going to sit, and marched straight to the back of the class where Stephen was seated. As Stephen, an 18-year-old African American male, laughed with his peers, Christina engaged in a major interruption: She jumped on Stephen's lap, threw her arms around his neck, and gave him, in dramatic fashion, a kiss on the lips and then one on each cheek. "Heeyyy there, Boo," is what Christina finally said to Stephen as he sat there with a look of utter shock on his face and paucity seemingly running through his stiffened, unmoving body. He offered no sign of reciprocated affection. He neither greeted her nor looked into her eyes, but she didn't seem to mind. "Y'all know this my boyfriend so don't be lookin' all surprised. I'm gettin' the love y'all don't got." When no one responded to her antics, she stated, "Lemme go 'head and get up. We'll talk later." She swung her body off of his body, and as if nothing had just transpired—Christina's antics, as students and I came to call them—Stephen returned to the conversation he was participating in with his peers. I stared at him as if to question: *Did you not feel Christina sitting on your lap? Did you not feel her kissing your lips and cheeks? Did you not feel violated? Did you not think you'd be implicated in her antics?* He looked at me, shrugged his shoulders, and turned back to his peers. Christina did not miss a beat, either. She walked up to me with hands on hip and said, "Sorry, Mizz, but sometimes you gotta do what you gotta do to prove a point. Anywayzzz, here's my homework, okay? It's an A cause I worked hard on it, okay."

And this is where this fifth chapter, "Cryin' for Christina," begins.

WHO'S CRYIN'?

After Christina hopped off of Stephen's lap and approached me, I stood there, my eyes moving back and forth from Christina to Stephen. As I contemplated my next move, I noticed that some students were sitting in their chairs chatting with nearby peers while others quickly strolled into the classroom. In 30 seconds (now 29, 28, 27 . . .), class was to begin, but I needed to address Christina's behavior, so I asked her to step into the hallway with me. I don't remember the exact hallway conversation Christina and I had on that Monday morning because over the course of our time together, we shared many moments in the hallway, sometimes talking about her behavior or her comments to other students, and at other times just staring at each other, trying to figure out our next move. Although I could write an entire chapter on Christina's "antics," what I find more fascinating was her comment, "Anywayzzz, here's my homework, okay? It's an A cause I worked hard on it, okay." This comment serves as the basis for the questions, vignettes, and discussions I offer around Christina's (as well as her peers') literacy engagements, dispositions, and academic as well as personal struggles.

To really get at—dig deep into, think critically about, and question—students' literacy engagements, this chapter poses the following questions: In what ways are literate identities taken up and performed by Christina and her peers? How do these identities both mask and reveal academic, personal, and social struggles? What are specific ways students work to un-silence dialogues on skills, process, and choice in order to begin critiquing "the culture of power" (Delpit, 1995, 1996) within schools and throughout society? What implications might this work—performing literate identities, un-silencing dialogues, interrogating power—have for people (e.g., students and teachers) and practices (e.g., in teaching and learning)?

In addressing these questions, this chapter briefly revisits Delpit's discussion of "other people's children" and "the culture of power," not as a way to relive the longstanding debate on skills versus process, but to think through deeper issues of power, miscommunication, and alienation experienced by some students of color in urban classrooms. From there, I offer two interrelated, thematic scenes that place Christina and her peers' academic realities and personal struggles center stage. First, I focus on examples of students' reading and writing activities that either speak to or speak against Christina's belief that simply doing schoolwork should constitute an A. Then, I describe selected forms of student participation as well as dispositions (stance, attitude, and resistances) toward school and schooling that were enacted in the classroom and that reflected other students' literacy engagements. Together, the examples presented in this chapter address academic and social conflict in the classroom in ways that bring to the forefront power and forms of alienation.

POWER AND PEOPLE'S CHILDREN

In *Other People's Children: Cultural Conflict in the Classroom*, Delpit (1995) discusses a variety of topics, from language diversity, multiculturalism and education, political implications of teaching, and learning literate discourses to educational, political, and cultural lessons learned in Papua New Guinea. She also addresses conflicting perspectives around utilizing a skills-oriented or a process-driven approach to teach writing to students of color. In so doing, she argues that explicit discussion on, and interrogation of, the culture of power has the potential to address larger issues involving alienation, miscommunication, and silence experienced by some students in classrooms. One way to address these conflicting perspectives, exacerbated by the "schism between liberal educational movements and that of non-white, non-middle class teachers and communities" (p. 24), is by recognizing power and the ways power can stimulate or avert equitable, democratic educational practices. Thus, Delpit identifies five complex components of power and hence of the culture of power:

1. Issues of power are enacted in classrooms.
2. There are codes or rules for participating in power; that is, there is a "culture of power."
3. The rules of the culture of power are a reflection of the rules of the culture of those who have power.
4. If you are not already a participant in the culture of power, being told explicitly the rules of that culture makes acquiring power easier.
5. Those with power are frequently least aware of—or least willing to acknowledge—its existence. Those with less power are often most aware of its existence. (p. 24)

Insofar as schools are concerned, Delpit's reference to the culture of power points to how the cultural capital of White and economically privileged (e.g., middle- to upper-class) students reflects the values of, practices in, and pedagogies associated with the educational system. On this latter point, she argues, "success in institutions—schools, workplaces, and so on—is predicated upon acquisition of the culture of those who appear in power . . . the culture of the school is based on the culture of the upper and middle classes—of those in power" (p. 25). This predication, particularly for many students of color and students from poor and working-class backgrounds, often creates a tense relationship between how one fits into, belongs, and identifies with values in school and nonschool contexts. For instance, in his autobiographical, or autoethnographical, text, *Voices of the Self*, Gilyard (1991) provides an analysis of the ways African American students are often forced to negotiate linguistic and cultural identities across seemingly conflicting contexts of schools and local communities. He writes: "I was torn between institutions, between value systems. And at times the tug of school was greater, therefore the 90.2 average. On the other occasions the streets were a more powerful lure, thus the heroin and the 40 in English." In Gilyard's case, he came to realize that there was "no middle ground or more accurately, no total ground on which anomalies like me could gather" (p. 160).

Undoubtedly, Gilyard is not alone in his recognition of the culture of power, and of how the values of that culture get enacted in ways that promote dangerous dichotomous relationships, or binary oppositions: school practices versus community values; "academic" language versus African American language, Spanish, and Spanglish; and professional identities versus personal identities. Accounts by Villanueva (1993), Kohl (1991), Anzaldua (2007), and others depict similar tensions with how cultural capital and the culture of power get taken up by, and through, middle- to upper-class values associated with established systems of education. Such accounts reveal a necessity for teachers, teacher educators, administrators, community members, and researchers to work with, and learn from, students in ways where power—its culture and representative codes—is questioned and critiqued in schools, classrooms, and throughout society. One way to do this, according to Delpit (1995), is by explicitly teaching students:

> The codes needed to participate fully in the mainstream of American life, not by being forced to attend to hollow, inane, decontextualized subskills, but rather within the context of meaningful communicative endeavors; that they must be allowed the resources of the teacher's expert knowledge, while being helped to acknowledge their own "expertness" as well; and that even while students are assisted in learning the culture of power, they must also be helped to learn about the arbitrariness of those codes and about the power relationships they represent. (p. 45)

In considering Delpit's suggestions, initially offered 17 years ago, and in reflecting on the experiences I shared with Christina and her peers in the English course at Perennial High School, I cannot help but to think about the pedagogical direction offered by Carter G. Woodson (1933/2011). In *Mis-education of the Negro,* Woodson insists that African American students be taught the canon of European ideological thought, that is, the language and literacy practices of the mainstream, or those in power. However, Woodson argues that this type of teaching cannot happen in isolation from education that involves the history, culture, and literacy traditions of African American people, given that "one finds little to show that Negro figures in these curricula" (p. 134). His stance concerning the education of African American students is clear: "In supplementary matter a good deed of some Negro is occasionally referred to, but oftener the race is mentioned only to be held up to ridicule. . . . How, then, can the school ignore the duty of teaching the truth while these other agencies [the press, media, general public] are playing up falsehood" (pp. 134–135)? His suggestion, in terms of teaching African American students, is even clearer:

We must find out exactly what his background is, what he is today, what his possibilities are, and how to begin with him as he is and make him a better individual of the kind that he is. Instead of cramming the Negro's mind with what others have shown that they can do, we should develop his latent powers that he may perform in society a part of which others are not capable. (p. 151)

Woodson's words are just as relevant today as when he first penned them in the 1930s. They are foundational for how contemporary scholars (Delpit, 1995; Gilyard, 1991; Haymes, 1995; hooks, 1989) center race and power in theorizations on, and practices related to, the education of African American students (and, I would add, other students of color) in and out of school contexts.

Taken together, sentiments from Woodson (1933/2011) and his contemporaries point to a fundamental message asserted by Delpit (1995), one that is either embraced, debated, or situated as a difficult task to actualize: "Teachers need to support the language that students bring to school, provide them input from an additional code, and give them the opportunity to use the new code in a nonthreatening, real communicative context" (p. 53). Doing this work, as my experiences at Perennial demonstrate, is more difficult than it appears, especially when an explicit, combined focus on the culture of power, school-sanctioned practices, students' prior knowledge, and Democratic Engagements stimulates feelings of alienation (from peers; from school) and miscommunication (with un/solicited participation; with meanings of academic achievement—"an A"). The performances of those feelings—alienation, miscommunication—as connected to silence and power, and as demonstrated through writing and participation, can heavily impact classroom literacy engagements. Nevertheless, an explicit focus on the culture and codes of power in the educational experiences of students of color has the potential to reveal "dominant ideologies, policies, and practices that are unjust" (Willis, Montavon, Hall, Hunter, Burke, & Herrera, 2008, p. 49).

LITERATE IDENTITIES

Building on Delpit's (1995, 1996) research on the culture of power and other people's children, this section turns the gaze to specific classroom scenarios. In the first scenario, I provide examples of Christina's (and her peers') literacy activities, which reveal beliefs about how *doing* academic work translates into academic achievement. As referenced in the beginning of this chapter, Christina assumed that the more she wrote, the better her grade would be, regardless of the line of argument, supporting evidence, presence of voice, and larger implications demonstrated (or not) in her writing. Thus, I ground the first scenario in Delpit's insistence that students be taught explicitly the culture and codes of power. Doing so has the potential to reveal deeper struggles some students have with *doing* school. The second scenario focuses on Christina and her peers' participation and dispositions toward each other and toward school in ways that reframe classroom conflict from disruptive, interruptive chaos to opportunities of engagement that might reveal feelings of miscommunication and alienation. In this reframing of conflict, it becomes important for teachers to see beyond and through the surface of things (see Chapter 2).

Christina's Writing About What?

During a class discussion on readings from *City Kids, City Teachers: Reports from the Front Row,* edited by Ayers and Ford (1996), students and I struggled with trying to pose a group definition of community. Our struggle had just as much to do with how we—a collective of about 27 people—conceptualized community in the geographical sense of the word as it did with how we understood and/or valued the histories, social dynamics, cultural resources, and political structures within communities. Although we had already spent more than a week reading and critiquing the various essays that comprise *City Kids, City Teachers,* we kept returning to the first paragraph of the "Foreword," written by Ossie Davis. It reads:

> To read this book is to get a sense of the siege—of children and of the cities in which they live under relentless attack. I feel the pain, and the anguish, and the fear, particularly in the words of children. Yet, I also find consolation, as well as inspiration and determination. The schools of America are where much of the war to redeem America must and will be fought. It's good for the soldier to know where the battlefield is. (p. xi)

Our constant return to this passage, thanks in large part to Damya, Aureliano, and Celina, indicated our search to understand "the siege," "the pain," "the anguish," and "the war to redeem" experienced by countless children and youth attending public schools across America. When we discussed Rodriguez's (1996) "Always Running," Haberman's (1996) "The Pedagogy of Poverty Versus Good Teaching," Jordan's (1996) "Nobody Mean More to Me Than You and the Future Life of Willie Jordan," and Delpit's (1996) "The Politics of Teaching Literate Discourse," among other readings, we loudly and energetically debated ways to improve, in the words of Haberman, "the quality of urban teaching" (p. 118). This point came through clearly when students interacted with pre-service teachers (see

Chapter 1). The debate led us to consider, and even disagree with each other on, meanings of teaching (especially with care and concern), reform, and accountability in schools located in poor and working-class communities.

As one of the students, Abana, declared: "When people say things like reform or improve teaching, they're talking about getting rid of bad teachers. That's part of the puzzle. The other part is asking us [students] what needs reformed. They're not doing that asking." Abana's comment was immediately followed by Hector's sentiments: "You not waiting for them to ask us, right?," which was followed by laughter that quickly turned serious. He continued: "Somebody said care. If they not asking us what needs reforming and how, we gotta ask if they care about us or trying to keep the structure, the system." Christina, who was sitting alongside some of her peers at a table to my left, and who was busily writing something in a notebook, interrupted the conversation and inquired, "What system y'all talkin' 'bout? Do y'all even know what y'all talkin' 'bout? Don't be stupid. GOSH" (capitalization reflects her verbal emphasis). Before I could address Christina's outbursts, it sounded as if a choir—off tune and singing different songs at the same time—had taken center stage. All I saw were heads turned toward Christina, and all I could hear were voices uttering remarks such as "Who you calling stupid, *stupid*?" "You don't read." "That's what's wrong with you now, girl." "Don't ever know what's going on." "Make me sick." Once again, Christina had succeeded in getting everyone off topic. I walked over to Christina and told her to come talk with me after class, and as I did, Jennifer said, "And Miss, don't be nice to her. She deserves what you got to give her. Please let her know she wrong."

Instead of remaining off-topic and directing unfriendly comments toward Christina, I invited everyone to participate in a collaborative writing task. That is, I wanted us to design a question or prompt related to arguments presented by the readings and student comments. Before I could explain the collaborative task, Christina interrupted and asked, "Can we come up with a question dealing with community, Mizz?" No one seemed to mind, and in fact, many students were shocked by Christina's suggestion. During the last 20 minutes of class, we tried to settle on a question. Christina, in many ways trying to redeem herself from her earlier remarks, walked to the board and wrote the word *community*. Next to it, she wrote "definition, examples, please." Then, she marched back to her seat.

Everyone took Christina's suggestion seriously, something students rarely did when Christina offered a direction for us to follow. In taking her seriously, we finally arrived at a possible prompt. Karimah raised her hand and asked if she could be in charge of writing the question on the board. As she came forward, students publicly exchanged ideas about community—what to ask, what it means, and what they wanted to consider and discover. Our 20 minutes on this task were just about up, but not before we agreed upon the following prompt: *How do you define community? In the definition, which better not come from a dictionary but yourself, write on personal connections to community and describe sites in the community you go to or walk past just about daily.*

During subsequent class sessions, students exchanged responses and received peer feedback (e.g., questions, directions, and examples to incorporate) in order to further develop their ideas. I recall Christina handing her response to me and asking for "an assessment, or a checkmark's fine, okay?" The following is an unedited excerpt from her response to the prompt on community:

> My neighborhood not so bad or to, to good. Its getting better than expected. Its just write. Know one gets hearts they anymore. They talk [illegible next word] and don't fight. I think. They use to be [illegible word that looks like "fight"]. They were good and bad things that was said and also happen in the neighborhood. But we have move on for the better and will do better. I wrote on neighborhood, maybe thats the same as community. Now you no my sites. I think, neighborhood need to be safe. If it's friendly not hostile like people hating each other, that a good neighborhood. This a short writing, but that's how I feel. I no its not clear. But this honest. Y'all go 'head judge me. I say what true.

It took me some time to read and comprehend Christina's entry, mainly because of an abundance of illegibly written words in both the above excerpt and in the longer response. Underneath Christina's word choices and forms—"write" for "right," "know" for "no," "hearts" for "hurt," "they anymore" for "there anymore," "its" for "it's," and so on—is a message of possibility. This message begins to surface in sentences such as "My neighborhood not so bad or to, to good. Its getting better than expected." Additionally, Christina claimed that "now you no my sites," when, in fact, she neither listed nor described any community sites. An evaluation of her writing, including her writing style, form, structure, choice of words, and levels of coherence, reveals a student who has not fully mastered the traditional codes and conventions of academic writing. However, and just as important, a closer examination of her written ideas shows a student who has a voice ("But we have to move on for the better and will do better"), who is expressing thoughts on paper ("This a short writing, but that's how I feel; I no its not clear. But this honest"), and who is grappling with feelings of miscommunication or being misunderstood ("Y'all go 'head judge me. I say what true"). Her writing leads me to wonder: Why has Christina, a high school senior, not mastered academic codes and conventions in ways that would allow her to assert a stronger academic voice?

When students participated in a peer exchange of writing during a follow-up class session, Christina walked over to Damya and asked, "You gonna read my paper, okay?" Damya was taken aback, probably because she and Christina have an antagonistic relationship, one defined by verbal interactions such as the following:

> *Christina:* Y'all stupid. Ain' no [none] of y'all
>   know what y'all talkin' 'bout.
> *Damya:* Girl, that's why no one likes you. You
>   really need to stop acting like that.
> *Christina:* You gonna make me?
> *Damya:* You don't want this, so stay away
>   from me . . . and don't sit by me.

Even with such interactions and similar others, Christina respected Damya, which was probably why she sought her out for the peer exchange. In my opinion, Christina believed Damya would engage in "a very special kind of listening, listening that requires not only open eyes and ears, but open hearts and minds" (Delpit, 1995, p. 46). She agreed to work with Christina, and upon reading her entry on the topic of community, Damya made the following suggestions (from my audio notebook):

> Let's get serious, Christina! Maybe you should give clear examples
> because examples always help me flesh out ideas. Give examples to
> answer the question and to let the reader see how you visualize things.
> Now, you say you've listed sites, but you don't. Go back and do that.
> If you can't think of sites, talk about the school . . . that's a site you
> go in almost every day. One more thing, but I need you to put your
> attitude aside for this one [Christina replies with a very soft, "Okay.
> Go 'head."] I'm not picking on you, but you should get help with
> your writing. You have good ideas, but you use the wrong words.
> There's a difference between "write" and "right." I'm not picking on
> you, just telling things *I think you should know at this stage in the
> game* [Damya's emphasis, as heard in her voice. Very softly, Christina
> confessed: "I know you right. I know."]

From this exchange, I asked students to revise, edit, and expand their ideas from the original response about community based on feedback from the peer exchange. Christina did not share her revisions with me until the following week (nearly 5 days later). When she did share her revised response, Christina aggressively handed it to me as she softly admitted to "getting tutoring help 'cause . . . I need some." The following passage represents Christina's attempts to both revise and extend on points from the original entry:

My neighborhood isn't so bad or good. Its getting better than
expected. Its just right. Know one gets hurts anymore. They talk
and don't always fight. I think. They use to be [illegible word]. They
were good and bad things that was said about the neighborhood.
But we have move on for the better and I hope we will do better.
I wrote on neighborhood, and that word means community from
how I see things. Now before I had no sites, but I no school is a site
I see everyday. I walk in the school for class, but I walk by it on the
weekend. I think, neighborhood like schools need to be safe. I don't
want people hating each other in the neighborhood and school. This a
short writing, but that's how I feel. Its not to clear cause I'm working
on it. I don't care if y'all judge me. I say what true. Now I mention
school as site. Let me talk on that. This week we talk on education in
class. Education is one of the best thing in the world that any person
could every learn. My education is not own par, but it's something
I got. I could have learned more if I was not so bad so many times.
But from what I did learn, I can open and run my own business
with it. I am a person that likes to have fun and play some times a
little too much, but I can take care of busses [business] and do those
things after. I got a lot to write and I was told I need to no certain
things now in my life [a reiteration of Damya's comment, *I think
you should know at this stage in the game*]. Education ties to school
and neighborhood. See, thats what I do in school and I take it to my
neighborhood. I no I'm not understood all times and I'm bad cause
nobody listen to me. If they do they gotta judge me. I don't like that.
But I'm a try. That's all, OK?

Christina's expanded journal entry focuses on the original prompt
about community, incorporates suggestions from Damya (e.g., offering examples and sites, referencing the school as a site, addressing word choice),
and introduces ideas around a topic (education) that the class was beginning
to more explicitly examine. In addition, her entry exposes larger issues that
she struggles with: being bad, having no one who listens to her, being misunderstood and judged, and needing to know "certain things at this point
in my life." Undoubtedly, Christina's "acting out" in class, marked by her
abrupt sitting atop her boyfriend's lap, calling other students stupid, and
constant interruptions and bantering, were not just behavioral issues. They
were performances of disruption marked by feelings of miscommunication,
alienation, and powerlessness. Her admission of being "bad" and "judged,"
things she "don't like," was a call for attention. Given that she regularly
sought these things out in class with no success, she decided to move beyond
searching for them and into directly asking for them—as was the case with
her straightforward question to Damya: "You gonna read my paper, okay?"

Delpit (1995) alludes to feelings of alienation and miscommunication in her discussion of the "silenced dialogue" and the culture of power. She argues that one comes to better understand these feelings "by seeking out those whose perspectives may differ most, by learning to give their words their complete attention, by understanding one's own power . . . by being unafraid to raise questions . . . and to listen, no, to *hear* what they say" (p. 47). Although Delpit is talking specifically about teaching, teachers, implicit and explicit acts of racism, and debates around pedagogical approaches to working with students of color ("skills" versus "process"), her points relate to Christina's dilemma with not being able to immediately access and use particular codes of power in an academic context. Nevertheless, Christina purposefully sought out Damya, someone whose perspectives appeared to differ from Christina's, and she accepted Damya's insights regarding ways to better express self in written form.

Near the end of the academic year (in June), about 3 months after the peer exchange, Christina volunteered to read excerpts of her writings to the entire class, something that she had never done before. As she stood up, she said, "Y'all need to shut it up. 'Cause y'all wanna hear what I gotta say." Unsurprisingly, her comment lead to disruption, and when she caught my eyes, she quickly apologized to everyone: "Okay, y'all know I'm bad. I guess I'm sorry for sayin' that, okay?" Juan, sitting closest to Christina, uttered, "She look serious. Go head, girl, I'll listen."

Christina asked to read three excerpts from different writing assign ments. She began by reading the questions, "Do you think it's valuable to study texts that have community as theme? Why or why not?" Then, she shared her response: "I . . . it's very good that the smarter your head is the higher you move up in life. The higher your life is, the better your com munity will be and can get. I . . . it all starts in the effort you put in to it first. You have to begin at knowing where to learn and go somewhere. That means knowing community is good. I wrote that in February." There were a few giggles in the room, to which Christina said, "Y'all know I doing this to show y'all I care, okay. I'm sorry for how I act." Silence followed her comment. Then, she read an excerpt from another text (note her emphasis on the emphasized words and phrases):

Why are some kids and parents discounted, and left to die? When 32 slaughtered on VA Tech campus, something is breaking down. *Money* is one of the main reasons. If people don't have money then they can't read, can't do much, don't wanta think rational. Then, *family efforts.* If your family is not all together then a lot of things you want to happen will not happen because you are not as close as you should be. Then *government funding.* The government might feel if you are trying for yourself why should they worry themself about you. I feel that if you want something done you have to try for yourself first because I know people don't jump up and care for you. Back to VA Tech. They left people to die on campus. See, I think if that was a black person who did that, his face would have been all over the news. But because the person was a nonblack and they said he killed hiself, he was not shown on the tv. This what I wrote after we read on the teacher who thought kids were making threats. The part when he [Jay Rehak, author of "Go Back and Circle the Verb" in *City Kids, City Teachers*] talked on "every child's vulnerability has led me to a special disdain for classroom violence."

Before allowing anyone to comment, Christina insisted on continuing, uninterrupted, with the third and final text. She framed her third text by talking about reading, writing, and establishing personal connections to texts. Then, she shared:

This one is an important topic. It is important to talk about Tupac in English class because he tells the truth about things going on. He tells us . . . he talks about family and how they try the best to help us, but sometimes its not enough. Because they might not have enough to help since they might be struggling themselves, or because they might not care enough about you. I know about that. And life, for example, if you say your going to do something and don't end up doing it, who gonna believe you next time around? We as a people gotta do better. [She inserted: I forget what I was going to write on that point. But let me finish.] Tupac tells it all, the good and the bad and the sad of each thing. Take for example a boyfriend and a girlfriend relationship. That can be looked at from many angles. I look at it like this: if you treat me good then I can return the favor. There is an old saying, "Do unto others as you want them to do to you." I really believe it, that the same way you treat me is the same way I will treat you. Tupac believe this cause he wrote about it in his songs eventho he lived by the motto "thug life." But that didn't mean he didn't care about people and community. He just had a hard life like me. That's why we should talk about Tupac in English class. I can relate to Tupac. [She inserted: Thank you. I'm done.]

Christina's sharing of sample writings with the class demonstrated a level of academic growth and maturity within the span of 3 short months. After she read her paragraph on studying texts that have community as a theme, she received a few giggles from her peers. Nevertheless, she did not "act out," "explode," or retreat into her familiar place of protection—a place that would have had Christina throw her papers on the floor, call everyone stupid, and proceed to the other side of the classroom door. Instead, she admitted to not being "a strong student, okay," which was a display of courage in the face of possible hostility. Her courage allowed her to share two additional writings with the class—one on violence and responsibility, and the other on studying Tupac Shakur and forming personal connections to him and to his work. These moments represented digressions from the scene described at the opening of this section on "Christina's Writing About What?" in that students did not feel completely under attack by Christina's words and actions: "Okay, y'all know I'm bad" (Christina); "She look serious" (Juan). Instead, they sat back, listened, and even looked at her with new eyes. As Carlos, a student who rarely spoken up in class, commented: "Why you don't let us see that side of you more? If you do, we'll know you better."

Seeing "that side" of Christina not only entailed a new way for students and me to view her, but also a new way for us to hear, notice, and receive her writing as process and product. Christina knew all too well that her writing, at least for an academic audience and for purposes associated with evaluation and assessment, was below a "12th grade place [status]." When Damya insisted that she "get serious," "give clear examples," and "get help with . . . writing," Christina took action by "getting tutoring help." Such action led to Christina's increased confidence level, which was exemplified by her decision to read excerpts of her writing in front of one of her harshest audiences—her classmates. I believe Christina's public reading signified the ways she began to grapple with issues of communication and miscommunication through writing—writing that involves a *process* by which to express and form connections to ideas, writing that gradually improves over time and practice, and writing that results in a *product* to be shared, critiqued, and revised.

Un-silencing Dialogues, but Not Before I Walked out of Class

In this next section, I offer examples of engagements, interactions, and projects in order to provide brief insights into student dispositions toward school and schooling. To do so, I frame the examples, or scenes, within excerpts from my unedited fieldnotes, which will paint a picture of specific moments of participation and their impact on students' academic and personal lives.

Scene 1, from my fieldnotes. So, class began in an untypical fashion. I don't know why I wrote untypical. Was it me with attitude? Was it my students not wanting to work on a Friday in March? Was it that we all had something or another on our minds that we thought was more important to do, act on, act out than the work we should have been doing? Where am I going with these notes? Wherever I head, I need to be honest about my role in class today. I can't believe I walked out, but I did.

I walked into a half full class. Gave Damya the digital recorder so she could get started with her video community project. Organized myself as quickly as I could—my bag, my papers, my mind—and asked students to organize themselves so we could start. Soon, I said something like, "Let's get started." I said it once. "Okay, everyone, let's get started." That was the second time I said it. I repeated myself a third time, a fourth time, a fifth, a sixth. Then I caught myself. "Am I the only one listening to me?" I didn't feel like waiting around anymore to get started. I gave a count-down?? What? C'mon! I looked across the room. Saw C [Christina] trying to get S [Stephen] to give her affection. I saw Victor showing a magazine to Rajon with feet propped up. Patricia was laughing with friends about something she did over the weekend. Everyone was doing something be-sides school, or so I assumed. The noise volume was too much. I said it again: "Let's get started." No one listened, and although they looked at me, they had no reaction. It went something like this [I eventually shared this paraphrase with the class]:

> *VK:* Let's get started. I've said this too many times already [as
> I reflect on these fieldnotes, I could see this scene in my
> mind, and I could hear my voice, which sounded like a
> record that was skipping back to the same three words].
> *Christina:* [Throws a big bag of snacks across the room and yells for
> someone to pick it up.] You betta get my bag off the flo [floor]
> and now. Who you playing with [talking to another student]?
> *Everyone:* [Talks over everyone else, including me.
> The talking continues, gets louder, and just simply
> increases. I think to myself that I've had enough.]
> *VK:* You know what, I'm not dealing with this today because
> obviously you don't want to deal with me. What's that about?
> *Everyone:* [Continues talking, getting up, laughing.]
> *VK:* Well, since no one wants to do school, no one wants to listen
> or at least tell me what's going on . . . [No one responded.
> So I picked up all of my things and said . . .] I'm out . . .
> not dealing with this for the period. We have less than 37
> minutes left, a lot to do, and no one wants to look at me.
> *Everyone:* [Stops talking and stares at me. I
> think I have their attention.]
> *VK:* Thank you. We can start [but that did not happen].
> *Christina:* Mizz, you can sit down. [C walks around the classroom
> as if she has a song playing in her head and a dance move
> about to emerge from her body. She asks for her bag of snacks
> back. She was so loud that all by herself, she sounded like

a choir complete with conductor, top tenors, and baritones,
and ready to give an encore even without a request.]

Everyone: [Looks at C and shakes their heads, but they all resume
talking, even louder than before. I've lost their attention.]

VK: [I walk toward the door, bag on shoulder and books in arms,
turn to them and say . . .] When you ready to work, get serious,
or let me know what's up, come get me. Until then, see you later.

I walked out of the classroom and into a nearby office. Inside, one of
my students, Abana, was talking with another teacher. Abana looked at me
and apologized for not being in class on time: "Miss Valerie, I'm sorry. I'm
on my way. I had to get something signed." To this, I abruptly told her that
it did not matter if she was coming to class or not because I was done for today and was not going back in. To this, I recall Abana emphatically saying,
"What! What happened?" Before I could think about responding to Abana,
she turned away and walked toward the classroom. Within 3 minutes or so,
Christina walked into the office and grabbed my arm. She acknowledged
her actions, apologized for them, "I'm sorry, Mizz," and asked me to return
to class, "I won't do it again. Come back, okay?"

We went back into the classroom only to meet one of the assistant prin-
cipals asking students what was going on. When I told her things would be
fine, she gave me a half-smile before leaving the room with a look of curiosity on her face. As she walked away, we could all hear the clashing sound
of metal from the keys gathered on her circular-shaped key ring holder; it
sounded as if a million keys were colliding, one onto the other. I closed the
door and sat my things down in this classroom—the same classroom out of
which I had recently walked. But this time, there was no noise, only silence.
I went in for it: "That is not happening again, and I mean it. The level of dis-
respect you showed me. And I'll be honest, I disrespected you when I walked
out. If we all check out that way, what's left? We have too much to do and
we need to do it with respect." I apologized and they did as well. But guess
what, by this time, the period was about to end. Man, oh man!

Reflections on walking. My walking out of class was a type of engagement with, or performance around, disruption. In other words, I sought to
disrupt disruption. I walked out of class because I was frustrated and because in order to both disrupt and interrupt the disruptions that were present—Christina's snack bag; Patricia's weekend recap; Victor and Rajon's
magazine hour; and so on—I needed to act, move, and participate within
the discourse that circulated in the room. Little did I know that this walking
out would become a pivotal moment for how students, especially Christina, recognized the disruptions. This recognition can be marked by Chris-

tina's approach and apology to me—"I'm sorry, Mizz"—which I assume was caused by something Abana said after she stormed into the classroom. Additionally, this walking out became significant for the types of honest confessions that followed: "You walked back in 'cause you care" (Rosa); "You all right, Miss" (Daniel); and "People walk out on me and don't ever walk back in" (Trina).

It was the latter confession by Trina that really caught my attention, especially since Trina never really talked up in class. Instead, she hid behind her long bangs and behind the presence of two of her friends, Aureliano and Jose. Nevertheless, my walking out allowed her to walk in insofar as her level of engagement with peers, with me, and even with course projects substantially increased. Over time, it became clear to me that Trina's feelings about schooling had a lot to do with her out-of-school, familial experiences: In both places, she felt alienated, alone, and misunderstood. Thus, her comment—"People walk out on me and don't ever walk back in"—was not simply an acknowledgment of my returning to the classroom and seeking to maintain teacher-student relationships, but of her feelings of abandonment that often do not result in people returning, apologizing, and staying. In other words, disrupting disruptions, at least in this case, led students (especially Trina) to publicly confront deeply seated feelings of alienation, miscommunication, and abandonment, as is evident in the below scene.

Scene 2, from my fieldnotes. I'm realizing a big change in Trina. Before, she was just so quiet that she wanted everyone to not notice her. But now, she's rocking our world. Understand, Trina seems so shy and bashful. She doesn't talk a lot in class—well, I should say she doesn't really talk up during class activities, but she does with her friends, like Aureliano and Jose. They can chat, chat, and chat. I remember in February or March when the seniors went on a class trip that she didn't go on. She came to my class. I think it was just me, Trina, and Rosa. From the brief experience with her, I was able to get a small glimpse into her life—into her inside realities. It was at this moment that Trina felt comfortable, for the very first time, talking to me about how her mother is strict and overly protective, to the point where she doesn't want Trina to go away to school. She said something about having dreams and wanting to do fashion design. But Trina's mother is like "No, that's not good enough" or is always asking her, "Who's gonna pay for that?" I was surprised that Trina shared this with me.

But in class today, Trina presented and talked about her father in terms of him abandoning her and her sister. She told all of us—her peers and me—that she has not seen him for over 14 years, although she's been told that he lives in close proximity to her. Everyone sat there, listening to Trina as she then said, without anyone prodding her, "He left us," "didn't say goodbye," "left all his things," and "never came back." The room fell silent.

Even Christina, who always had something off topic to say, sat there speech-less. Trina looked at all of us and said, "He and my mom were arguing and he ran out," "Sometimes I just wanna run away," "go and hide forever." Someone in the class, I think it was Abana, said, "Me, too." When Trina said, "Where are our fathers? They always leave us. We have to raise our-selves with our mothers," Michael, under his breath, but loud enough for everyone to hear him, commented, "I know. We can relate." This was such a raw moment—powerful, honest, insightful, and straight-up painful. For me, it just speaks to the many challenges students go through in their out-of-school lives that definitely impact their in-school lives and the ways some teachers and peers (mis)read their actions and identities.

No wonder Trina's mother is so protective. No wonder Trina seems to constantly wear sadness and misery on her face, even when talking with her closest classmates. No wonder. I have another type of respect, a heightened appreciation, for Trina and for all of my students. Always coming to see them with even more clear eyes, from day to day. After class and halfway into 4th period, I went looking for Trina. I pulled her out of class with her teacher's permission to ask for her project's poems. She gave them to me. We talked for a few minutes, and when we were finished, I kneeled right there in the hallway to document my memory of our conversation, which I shared (member checked) with Trina the very next day:

> *VK:* You're sitting on so much talent.
> *Trina:* [Laughs and seems to be bashful]
> *VK:* Why don't you shine more?
> *Trina:* I don't know. It's hard, with everything to think about.
> *VK:* And not just school, right?
> *Trina:* Yeah.
> *VK:* Can I ask you something?
> *Trina:* What?
> *VK:* Your father left. How do you now feel about it?
> *Trina:* Sad still. Always been. Don't know how I'll feel if I see him.
>   Been 14 years. He lives close, but he left us to struggle and
>   be alone. I've always missed him. But it's been 14 years.
> *VK:* Do you write about any of this? In a journal or . . . ?
> *Trina:* Actually, I do have a journal I write in all the time. I write
>   ideas and feelings. It's also filled with short stories and poems.
> *VK:* I'd love to see some of it one day . . . if that's all right.
>   I'd love to spend some time with you to get to know
>   more about you and your writing. Just let me know.
> *Trina:* That's fine. I'll bring my journal and we can maybe talk.
> *VK:* If you ever need help with class, let me know. You have
>   "it" and you just need to recognize it for yourself.
> *Trina:* I'll try. Maybe.

Reflections on Trina. Trina's discussion of her father abandoning his family stemmed from our examination of Bill Ayers's essay, "A Teacher Ain't Nothin' But a Hero: Teachers and Teaching in Film." Although it took some time for the class to get through the essay and make larger connections to the references Ayers presents (the essay appeared in *City Kids, City Teachers* in 1996 and I was teaching high school seniors in 2007), we were able to have honest, yet difficult conversations around media representations of teaching and teachers. Little did I know that Ayers's closing passage, which I include below, would strike a chord with Trina:

> Real teachers need to question the common sense, break the rules, become po-
> litical and activist in concert with kids. This is true heroism, an authentic act of
> courage. We need to take seriously the experiences of youngsters, their sense-
> making, their knowledge, and their dreams—and particularly we must inter-
> rogate the structures that kids are rejecting. In other words, we must assume
> an intelligence in youngsters, assume that they are acting sensibly and making
> meaning in situations that are difficult and often dreadful, and certainly not of
> their own making. In finding common cause with youngsters, we may also find
> there our own salvation as teachers. (pp. 239–240)

On the one hand, Ayers is talking about popular, one-sided narratives of teachers as heroes that get depicted in film, and on the other hand, he is calling for courageous, real teachers to recognize the experiences of young people "in situations that are difficult and often dreadful." Trina connected to the above passage in a very personal way. She read Ayers's words as she tried to make sense of her father's abandonment, and as a result of her reading, she asked me if she could reflect on the above passage in a class project. I asked Trina to write a description of a possible project that she wanted to complete, and to submit it to me within 3 days. She submitted 3 different ideas:

1. I'd like to write about a song, "Lithium," which is about not wanting to be alone and wanting to be free of depression. This song reminds me of my childhood and how my dad left me and my sister. I can use the song as the basis to write about being courageous and seeing my strength through the sadness. I'll relate it to the readings we've done, especially to William A [Ayers].
2. Another song that comes to mind is a song titled, "Hello." This song reminds me of my childhood when I was struggling without friends and I couldn't talk at all because I was just too scared. Then I got a voice, but I'm still working on making my voice louder. I see this connecting to what we've been reading

on seeing young kids' intelligence by not rejecting people and showing care. I want to combine the other idea [#1] with this [#2] and write an essay with a central theme. I'll use class readings, and I might even sing my paper to the class.

3. I'll be honest. What I really want to do is a project about my daddy and the way I express my feelings toward my daddy. I express my feelings for him by playing a song called "Hello," as well as others because these songs are really sad and that's how I feel about him leaving me. After reading that guy's long essay [Ayers] and when I'm done doing this project, I think I will calm down about how I really feel, which I have never told anyone. I've written about my feelings to myself, but never shared them. Maybe I can do something like this for a project for you, even if it's an extra project you give me feedback on and not a grade.

Instead of making this a major class project, Trina decided to write a poem and a reflection about her father. Eventually, she gained enough courage to present her writings to the class. On the day of her ungraded presentation, I could tell that she was nervous, and it appeared as if her friends, Aureliano and Jose, were equally nervous. She awkwardly stood before the class and read the following:

"Daddy's Little Girl"

When I was daddy's little
Girl, I would run into
His arms.
When I was daddy's little
Girl, I never felt alone.
When I was daddy's little
Girl, I would always go
On adventures with
Him around the City.

When I was daddy's little
Girl, me and my dad would
Draw whatever comes into
Our minds.
When I was daddy's little
Girl, he would tuck me
Into bed and tell me,
"I love you, daddy's little girl."

The applause was thunderous, and served as encouragement for Trina to read her second piece:

"My Father"

When I look into the mirror, I sometimes see my father and I start to think how much I miss him and how much fun we had together. Before he left me and my sister, I would remember all the good times we had together like riding our bikes in the park, playing Super Nintendo when my mom was not at home, draw together, and take naps together. When my father left, I felt half of myself leaving with him and never returning back. Sometimes I would hate my father for not being there as I got older but then most of the times, I just did not care or pretended to not miss him. I just wish he would just see me one last time and I'll show him how much I love him.

Students asked Trina various questions, including, "What assignment is this? Did I forget to do it?" When someone asked her about her intentions with doing this project, Trina talked about wanting to understand how someone could abandon family. This response was an opening that allowed me to further inquire into the larger motivations behind Trina writing the poem and reflection. To this, Trina responded: "There's something inside William A's words that make me feel a certain way." She went to her table, retrieved the book, and read a part of Ayers's passage, cited above. She placed extra emphasis on phrases such as "authentic act of courage," "interrogate the structures," and "assume that they are acting sensibly and making meaning."

Christina wondered aloud about Trina's abandonment by saying: "Okay, I relate. I can't see how they up and leave. I think on that often, I never talk it up, though. Leaving me affected my actions. I'm bad but what else I'm suppose to be?" She continued, "I didn't know we share something [looking at Trina]. We don't like each other much, but I'm glad you did the project. I don't want to be bad anymore."

Through her project, Trina exposed feelings that were at the root of some students' personal experiences: feelings associated with abandonment, miscommunication, and alienation. While I know that the root causes of such feelings are not explicitly discussed in Delpit's (1995) book, I do contend that her sentiments on the culture and codes power in educating students of color are attentive to the problem of "the silenced dialogue." This "silenced dialogue" is not just about skills versus process, the ways White teachers teach African American students, and the exclusion of perspectives on pedagogy by African American teachers and other teachers of color. It, "the silenced dialogue," is also about what some teachers do not see, or fail to acknowledge and encourage inside of classroom spaces. These things include the connectedness of class texts to students' personal, analytic readings of those texts; the role of voice and choice insofar as how students process information and reflect on their own lived conditions and shifting identities; and the tools, or codes, that allow students to take up this academic and personal work in nonthreatening, yet critical contexts.

It is the reliance, by many teachers, on "the silenced dialogue" that does not engage students as "experts on their own lives" by encouraging them to meaningfully engage academic work in ways relative to who they are, how they feel, and how they can become "authentic chroniclers of their own experiences" (Delpit, 1995, p. 47). Doing so might result in more teachers realizing the need "to question the common sense, break the rules, become political and activist in concert with kids" (Ayers, 1996, p. 239). Such points reiterate Woodson's (1933/2011) plea for teachers to discover the possibilities of students, particularly Black students, in order to critically teach them and help them negotiate ways to do school in light of a plethora of personal and political dilemmas.

MOVING OUT OF SILENCE AND WORKING THROUGH STRUGGLES

Throughout the senior-level English course, I attempted to facilitate collaborative relationships with, and among, students. It was my hope that doing so would encourage them to openly grapple with course texts, assignments, and one another in the classroom. Although it may appear as if Christina and her peers were not performing literate identities, I contend that they were doing so in ways reflective of academic and personal struggles that were grounded in their utilization or non-utilization of the codes of power. The examples of Christina's reading and writing, her aggressive attitude toward her peers, and the association she made between feelings of alienation and miscommunication across school and community contexts reveal levels of conflict that hardly ever get addressed within classrooms, even when they are visible indicators of disruption.

To say it another way, teachers are not only educating "other people's children," but our very own—students who come to see teachers with a certain peculiar gaze, who come to rely on or dismiss our knowledge, and come to view school as either an empowering place or as an institution equipped with alienating structures that are not named for what they are. To name these structures is to explicitly call them codes of power that "are enacted in classrooms," that serve as "rules for participating in power," and that "are a reflection of the rules of the culture of those who have power" (Delpit, 1995, p. 24). To not name them as such is to ignore the inequitable structures that are already in place when students, particularly poor and working-class students and students of color, enter into schools to learn, to engage in process, and to play with product.

Equally important is that students in the English course came to embrace their struggles and name the reasons behind their feelings of alienation
and miscommunication. In Trina's case, she acknowledged that her sadness
was a direct result of her father's abandonment. For Christina, she recognized that being "bad" stemmed from feelings of loneliness she encountered
in and out of school. Such confessions, paired with representative student
writings and engagements, point to critical issues with teaching and learning
that move beyond my one class. To move this work beyond my class requires that we interrogate those academic spaces in which power is present,
but not explicitly discussed, and where disruptions exist, but are not taken
up as texts to be performed and critiqued. Hence, revisiting "the silenced
dialogue" could prove meaningful for the ways conflict, miscommunication,
learning, and power impact classroom literacy engagements and students'
perceptions of school and schooling.

CHAPTER 6

Beyond Classroom Teaching

Literacy and Social Justice in the Library Foyer

Throughout *Crossing Boundaries,* I have presented examples that are specific to students' literacy engagements, activities, and identities in ways that I hope will impact aspects of critical teaching and learning. Beginning in the first chapter, evidence of teaching and learning as reciprocal acts and activities among teacher education candidates and high school students revealed larger questions related to diversity and equity in education that were either addressed in subsequent chapters in this book or that I continue to mull over on a daily basis. The range of these questions, while not exhaustive here, includes: What are some of the "multi-disciplinary understanding[s] of language, literacy, and pedagogy" (Cochran-Smith & Lytle, 1999, p 16) that impact student-teacher engagements, but from multicultural perspectives that center equity, diversity, and difference? How might students and teachers collaborate on efforts to establish a "common ground" in daily interactions within as well as beyond school spaces? In what ways might a reversal of learning positions—students as teachers; teachers and teacher education candidates as students—heighten literacy interactions and meaning making processes while fostering a sense of community, responsibility, reciprocity, and Democratic Engagements? What do students think about existing school structures and learning processes? What would they change in, or about, the current educational push for academic excellence and achievement in leaving no child behind?

From here, the second chapter sought to give attention to particular cases at Perennial High School such as the local, historical context of East Harlem, the community where Perennial is located, and the spatial context of the actual school and curricular designs of the course I taught there. It was in this chapter that I highlighted our consorted efforts—high school students and me—to co-design, or reshape, the guiding curricular goals for the course in ways that aligned with New York State standards for grade 12 English. The four learning goals, or standards, are representative of lessons in social interaction, information gathering and understanding, literary expression and response, and critical analysis and evaluation. Although I may not have directly paralleled the ways such goals and standards connect to the featured student work and experiences within representative chapters,

I believe that the connections are quite visible. For instance, students were invited to grapple with topics of school conditions and community change (recall students' reactions to the Taylor quote included on the course syllabus in Chapter 2), as well as identity, power, and democracy (remember Celina's comment that "what we got in this country ain't a democracy" in Chapter 3). They were also invited to question issues of belonging and freedom (consider Rosa and Aureliano's musical performance on themes of love, abandonment, and identity in Chapter 4), and feelings of alienation, miscommunication, and academic (under)preparedness (Christina's antics in Chapter 5). Thus, I argue that such interactions were grounded in the critical ways students analyzed ideas related to their own shifting identities, academic practices, literacy resistances, and state-sanctioned standards. Students' engagements across components of literacy and in the face of disruptions and interruptions (see Chapter 5) point to meaningfully rich, timely, and relevant encounters that required them to read, write, listen, and speak with, and for, purpose.

While these interactions occurred within the specific classroom context in which I worked at Perennial, they have wide-reaching implications for other teaching and learning moments across various spaces. As I noticed at the school, such interactions emerged in hallway, cafeteria, and stairwell conversations shared among multiple students and teachers; in the civic engagements people had within community spaces; in discussions at the school and in the local community around democratic participation in the United States; and in people's public wonderings about positive, enduring attempts at coalition building within the local environment and across more global (e.g., geographical, virtual) settings. Implications point to, but are not limited by, the educational significance of crossing boundaries (e.g., students and teacher education candidates, students to students, students and classroom teachers) and the urgency with which students and teachers should confront fears, biases, presuppositions, and power structures as related to education, specifically within urban contexts.

With these realities in mind, I am left to reflect on larger consequences of this work insofar as processes of teaching and learning in urban public schools are concerned. Specifically, I cannot help but to imagine rewriting curricular standards in ways that center children's and young adults' voices, perspectives, and literacy lives. Doing so might result in increased levels of responsibility and commitment to education by, for, and because of young people. In addition to rewriting standards with students, I argue that an explicit focus on literacy as connected to democracy and to the history of Black and Brown people as readers and writers in and across the United States can contribute to an educational design constructed upon multicultural principles, equitable practices, and culturally relevant pedagogies.

In my current international work, supported by a Fulbright-Hays award to Sierra Leone, West Africa, a group of K–12 public school teachers, doctoral students, and university professors from South Carolina and I are collaborating on the development and dissemination of curricula that might help teachers, teacher educators, and students in elementary, middle, and high schools gain a stronger understanding of connections between Sierra Leone and the United States. Our hope, among so many others, is that the ties that bind people together across the Atlantic will become more visible in pedagogical practices, professional development opportunities, and curricular reform efforts. Without an intentional focus on these connections, ones that are guided by historical, cultural, and linguistic components, especially as they relate to education, I fear that any attempt at school reform will fail. In addition to these specific components and to international work that explores curricular approaches and historical associations, there are other factors that we must attend to. These include establishing strong school-community partnerships, inter- and cross-disciplinary educational collaborations, and training programs focused on teacher education candidates' performances and interactions in classrooms where the majority of students, who are of color and from poor and/or working-class backgrounds, are often assigned.

Clearly, teachers, teacher educators, and literacy researchers should, actually must, work alongside students to co-create meaningful opportunities to experiment with various interpretive, analytical behaviors. Thus, conversations on what Delpit (1995) refers to as complex components of power, or "the culture of power," can become visible as students and teachers take on Royster's (2000) insistence to "construct ways of being, seeing, and doing in recognition of the materiality of the world around us and of who and how we are in our sundry relationships to it" (p. 284).

Indeed, the demands and ensuing consequences I allude to are large; in no way can they be reasonably answered with a single narrative or a set of scripted suggestions. I do not pretend to have definitive answers for them. What I do believe, however, is that such demands should not be addressed by proposing more legislative mandates or one-size-fits-all programs that purport educational advancements for students of color. In many cases, such attempts reiterate longstanding racist and classist systems grounded in unfairness, exclusion, and inequity. Therefore, my goal with this last chapter is to offer ideas, which I am still developing and (re)considering, that place positive attention on the engagements young people are already having in schools. Such engagements, which adults sometimes overlook or ignore, are not particularly a part of the official (or hidden) curriculum, but are a part of students' daily interactions across school contexts. In what ways, then, might these student-initiated, student-sponsored engagements enhance teaching and learning as these relate to school activities, structures of power, and educational practices and policies? Recall Quinton's declaration, "SCHOOL'S BORING, SCHOOL'S BORING, and oh yeah, did I say SCHOOL'S BORING. WHAT YOOOUUU EXPECT," and Alexandria's frustration with "get[ting] tired of having to do the same thing all the time in classes." In recalling these sentiments from students, let us swiftly move closer to recognizing the "authentic," self-selected literacy engagements of young people in relation to teaching practices and legislative dictates.

"IS THIS LITERACY?" LEARNING IN THE LIBRARY FOYER

In the remainder of this chapter, I highlight specific examples of students' "authentic" literacy engagements within the context of Perennial. In particular, I examine scenes in which students voluntarily gathered in the makeshift space of the library lounge, or foyer, during the early mornings to prepare themselves for the daylong journey into and out of various classes. The exchange of ideas, critical disagreements, reading of news stories, and analyses of popular community events served to mark the library foyer as an unofficial site of critical engagement where students often participated more with literacy there than in some of their classes. In other words, the foyer served as an unsuspecting place—for some teachers and administrators—of students' literacy and social justice interactions. This chapter points to possibilities of classrooms becoming like the foyer in terms of student engagement, talk, and involvement with interpreting, analyzing, and critiquing arguments and texts. In thinking about these possibilities, I offer reflections on how students encouraged me to consider the space of our classroom in ways similar to the space of the library foyer. My reflections take me to a place where questions of pedagogical practices and teaching with care surface.

Excerpts from my fieldnotes. I went to the main office to make copies of handouts for class this morning. The line was too long, moving too slowly. I figured I'd go on to the library to use the copy machine. Glad I did. There's like a little open area leading to the locked door that gets you into the library. I guess I can call this area a foyer or corridor or something. I'll say it's a foyer, something like a little nook area that has a few tables and chairs. There's also a door that'll lead into the nurse's office. I've been wondering if that was the nurse's office. I'd see Alexandria sitting in there from time to time, smiling with the nurse on duty. Sometimes she'd be in there sitting in a defensive position. But I do think she likes the nurse, just depends on the day, conversation, or reason why she's in the office. Well, today inside this foyer area were some students—Karimah, Rosa, Yvette, and about three others. I could tell that students were also inside the library, maybe for class, because when I went up to the library door, I peered into the little narrow glass that lets you see into the library, and there they were (note to self: Is the glass really as narrow as I think it is? I need to check on that). But no one came to open the door for me. Oh well! It didn't matter. I wanted to talk with my students in the foyer anyway.

Students told me Christina had just stormed off in tears, and Rosa said, "I'm just letting you know 'cause I'll bet she gonna be a hot mess in class today." I think those were my words—hot mess—but it pretty much sums up what Rosa was saying about Christina. I glanced at her, and recognized that look she was giving me, as if to say, "You best be prepared." I shook my head up and down to signify that I got the message. I took a seat at the table—there were about three roundtables in this foyer area—and as soon as I did, Karimah said, "Yeah, Miss Kinloch, sit right on down with us." She told me that I was the perfect person to be part of the current conversation about campus violence. I recall her asking if I'd heard about the shooting at Virginia Tech. Her question to me was quickly followed up with, "What's going on? Makes you not want to go off to college." Other students raised similar points about not going away to college during scary and violent times.

Yvette was sitting to my left, Rosa across from her, Karimah in front of me, and Robert by Karimah. Two guys were sitting at a table to my left, and another guy was sitting near Rosa. Yvette was hunched over reading the *Daily News* and its article about the campus shooting. Karimah wanted to know the gunman's motive and everyone uttered some version of, "Ah dunno," including me. She asked about the race or ethnicity of the person who did it, and when she asked, she turned her head in a downward position to locate the information in the article: "It might be in here, but maybe not." Yvette scooted closer in to me, still in a hunched over position, and said, "They tell us. I read it." She pointed to one section of the news story—"Here it is. No, not there"— and then to another section—"Here it says Asian male" and "distraught." As Yvette said that, she looked up at all of us and questioned why race was so important. She quickly added that people get so preoccupied with race and ethnicity. From her look, I could tell she was genuinely asking the question about racial significance, but no one at the table had an immediate answer for her. We thought about her question with one another, coming up with more reactionary responses as opposed to anything else. Someone said something like, "It's how things get represented." Someone else said, "Some people assume who'd do it," and yet another person said, "I just want to know. That's something we ask all the time." Yvette became more intentional when she inquired into why race mattered so much. To this, I remember Rosa's observation that it's how other people see you—"as Black or Latina"—even if they don't know you beyond what they think they see. Hence, the fascination with the perpetrator's race or ethnicity.

I was fully involved in the conversation, and couldn't help but to ask how they'd respond to violence or how they'd help someone else respond to it. I truly wanted to hear what they had to say about this. Karimah was really upset about the campus shooting, and said that there's no place for that kind of stuff in our lives. I recall her direct question back at me: "Why we gotta act like that? Tell me why." I searched in my heart and mind for an answer, but I was just as numb and dumfounded as anyone else. All I could say in that moment was, "I just dunno." Then they looked at me. Were they looking at me as a teacher who should have immediate answers? Were they looking at me the way people look at friends or family members who had suddenly become strangers in their eyes? What did I have to lose besides everything, and in knowing this, I still had to ask Karimah to talk to me about her look. "You human, too," is what she offered. "I mean, like, there's things even teachers don't have answers for. You being real."

Ohhh boy, a significant teachable moment was staring me in the face. I was glad for it. It positioned me as a student and Karimah and other students as teachers. I asked Karimah to talk to us about her reaction, tell us what was running through her mind. Rosa added into my request, asking Karimah what she'd do in this situation. What Karimah said will always stay with me. Her words have become cornerstones in my personal and professional life. She talked about people standing for something meaningful and positive. That we need to learn how to "love each other, even if we don't know each other that much or at all." Karimah passionately talked about being strong when we reach "a place of depression or frustration, or hatred and self-loathing." She said, "we gotta look at ourselves in the mirror and ask if things that bad," or if we "gonna make things worse and hurt people." Even more powerful was her statement about taking responsibility for our actions because "it ain't all about one person, what we do affects a lot more people than we could ever realize."

My eyes were welling up with tears. I was speechless. We were all moved and motivated. One look at my watch took me within a little less than 5 minutes before the beginning of class, with still no copies of handouts made. But it didn't even matter. We sat at that roundtable in silence, all of us, and Rosa broke the silence when she reached for a hug. Yvette reached across the table, trying to give her one. Rosa came to give Karimah one, and after they embraced, Karimah gave Robert a hug. She looked over at the guys sitting close by. They all stood up and gave hugs. The guys pretended to not care or want the hugs, but they took them and gave 'em right back. All of a sudden, they all turned and looked at me. I stood up, we hugged, tried to conceal unconcealable tears, smiled, and walked to class.

BREAKING THROUGH: ON NOT RELYING ON ASSUMPTIONS

The above excerpts from my fieldnotes reveal some of the emotional responses students and I had upon learning about the campus shooting at Virginia Tech. However much our conversation focused on that unfortunate, violent event and its impact on people far and near, our exchanges in the foyer were also about something more than violence and someone being labeled "distraught." We found comfort in that shared space and around a shared text. Students took ownership of, and interest in, the exchanges we had—from reading aloud self-selected passages from the news article, to scanning the article for responses to questions we all raised and recalling information about the reported events. In this particular school space (the library foyer), one in which students would informally and organically gather throughout the day, lessons emerged that required us to question intentions, express feelings, confront emotions, and search for connections that tied humans one to another in the name of solidarity.

When everyone finally entered the classroom—students who were gathered in the foyer, students who were not—I paused. I looked across the room and noticed some students laughing, some students with heads on the table, other students walking from one side of the room to another, and a few students slowly and unapologetically walking through the door. I thought about the engagements I participated in with Yvette, Karimah, Rosa, Robert, and the other male students sitting in the foyer. I remembered the solemn looks, the tears, and the hugs. Instantly, my present memories were interrupted. Students began asking what we were doing in class, whether homework was actually due, and if they would have time to work with writing partners.

Instead of following the planned routine, I said that we were going to spend the first half of class journaling about a topic, and the second half of class talking about our responses to the topic. Victor had a puzzled look on his face, and asked, "What topic?" Karimah looked up at me, and I asked if she had a topic in mind that she wanted us to consider. "C'mon, man. This stupid," and "She ain't got nothing," were some of the reactions offered from students. "Anything?" Karimah inquired, to which I said, "Anything." Karimah turned to the entire class and spoke over those who were talking with friends. She said: "This is what I think we should write on: What are you afraid of and how do you deal with being afraid without harming other people?" Victor wanted to know her motives for the question, and Karimah said, "Did you look at the news? Or even read the paper? If so, you'd be thinking Virginia Tech University." Silence followed, and students began journaling.

During the second part of class, I invited students to share some of their writings. Victor, to my surprise, volunteered to read. Here is an excerpt from his journal entry:

> Karimah, I did hear about VA Tech. I don't know if you have friends or anything there. I hope you don't but if so, I hope they're safe. What I'm afraid of is failure. This might sound funny, but I'm afraid to fail. Too many people in my life have failed me, and I hope I don't fail them. Maybe I can give them something to hold on to.

Daniel added: "Graduating high school because I don't know where I'll go. People think everybody has a plan they can pay for. I don't." Then, Christina raised her hand and read the following lines from her journal:

> Afraid? Like, I, afraid of afraid. Y'all know how I be acting. I can't control it all of the times. I'm working on it. Part of that's me being afraid of afraid. That don't make no sense, right? That's what I'm afraid of, tho. I act out to make y'all think I don't have fear, like I'm not afraid of things. But I am. Who ain't?

Sharif chimed in and directed his opening comment to Christina: "Put that energy into good and something good might happen." He shuffled with his loose paper and then read:

> There's a lot to be afraid of. The dark, the light, walking around a corner not knowing who's waiting for you, and a broken heart. Forgetting the past, feeling like you getting far away from memories of the people who passed away that you love. What's not scary these days? The thing about being scared is that you should also be able to say the things you're not afraid of. Smiling at someone not knowing if they even looking at you, telling your momma you love her, telling your father or uncle or your brother or a male in your life you want to be like them. Dreaming about the future and seeing yourself in it. Treating people with respect and not being afraid when they give that respect back to you. There's a lot to be afraid of, but also a lot to not be afraid it. It's an interesting balance you need to maintain.

Sharif's journal, as with the other ones highlighted above, conveyed powerful and personal messages that are often not shared within classroom contexts. In fact, their messages are often absent from the experiences that comprise instructional agendas and pedagogical practices. Yet their sentiments are important to solicit and recognize in attempts to foster meaningful teaching and learning relationships with students. How can we continue to overlook students' feelings and thoughts that indicate that many of them are "afraid of afraid," or "afraid to fail," or afraid of "getting far away from memories of the people who passed away that you love"? In what ways might teachers and teacher educators closely listen to the narratives students share—about themselves, their literacy practices, communities, and reactions to local and national events—in ways that offer openings into topics of identity, power, justice, struggle, and belonging? Are these topics not already central to the academic work in which we engage students and beckon them to complete? Might there be space in the curriculum for the inclusion of students' and teachers' subjective, emotional, and human reactions to real-life situations? In making space, might we be able to acknowledge the ways student reactions, through writing and discussion, point to specific measures they are required to meet, according to state standards?

For example, as students in the foyer were reading and discussing the news story, they were displaying abilities to use literacy for social interaction. During a follow-up session in the foyer a few days later, students had copies of other local and national newspapers that carried the story of the Virginia Tech shooting. Students made references to coverage from the nightly news, and had printed copies of articles on school violence that had occurred in other states within the last few years. These things represent information gathering and understanding. The journal writing and discussion session and the eventual connections students made between their journals and the various spoken-word poetry selections we had discussed in class point to literary expression and response. The ways they responded to each other's writings and reactions as well as solicited input from me serve as examples of their skills in critical analysis and evaluation. The point that I am trying to make here is that students—in the library foyer and the English class—were engaging the state learning standards in ways that were critical, insightful, and meaningful for them. Why, then, do we not tap into these moments—ones that occur in library foyers, cafeterias, on sidewalks that line school buildings, in schoolyards, and in other spaces that are beyond classrooms—as we engage teaching and learning with, and because of, students?

"AFRAID OF AFRAID": CLOSING SUGGESTIONS

In bringing this book to a close, I admit that I am still thinking through some of the dilemmas posed by this work (e.g., teaching demands; teachers working with four or more classes of students, some of whom might be on or below grade level; existing challenges against teachers as public employees with collective bargaining rights). I am also working through some of the possibilities (e.g., students as teachers, teachers as facilitators, students and teachers disrupting and interrupting the regular routine of classroom practices, students interpreting assignments within familiar examples). This final chapter opened with me thinking through lingering questions specific to students, teachers, and teacher educators working toward a "common ground" (Sharif), engaging in a reversal of learning positions, and fostering community. In thinking about these factors, I sought to acknowledge realities of teaching and learning in public schools, especially as these things relate to learning standards, teaching demands, and codes of power.

Clearly, I continue to work toward, build on, and grapple with the abovementioned factors, knowing that I am indebted to the lessons I learned from students at Perennial and in the other schools and communities into which I have been invited. I close this book by briefly highlighting some of the lessons that I have learned and that I continue to ponder in my own theoretical, conceptual, and practice-oriented work:

- Approaching teaching as a reciprocal act, where teachers teach students, and students teach teachers in ways that are facilitative. We can no longer approach teaching as a one-sided act or activity where "the teacher issues communiqués and makes deposits and students receive such deposits (Freire, 1970/1997, p. 57). This outdated approach is grounded in an unbalanced power relationship that does not invite students into the experimental, inquisitive nature of learning.
- Understanding that teaching content does not have to translate into routine "Do Now" activities, worksheets, or testing drills. As students have shown me, teaching content should include a variety of texts, experiences, and learning encounters generated by students and teachers and from schools and communities.
- Learning multiple ways by which to effectively model for students, and have students model, for teachers and their peers, critical skills and practices. The purpose of such modeling is not to privilege a particular discourse style or way of thinking, but to expose multiple ways by which to embrace, or wear, interpretive, analytical attitudes. In some ways, when teachers and students model critical skills and practices, which might serve to highlight aspects of critical thinking, the transferability of skills from one context to the next might result, even in messy, complex stages.
- Helping to foster a balance between skills and process approaches to teaching and learning. I think that such debates take time away from the teaching and learning that need to happen inside of public school classrooms. Such dichotomous relations—either skills or process, either left or right, either right or wrong—are a disservice to the diverse perspectives

and learning styles of students who sit in front of us on a daily basis. Can we find ways for our practices to embody diverse and different teaching approaches in ways that begin with what students expect to learn, ask to learn, and need to learn?

- Being explicit about the codes and the culture of power that operate within schools and throughout society. Although this sounds like an old argument that I am resurrecting, it is not. Power structures and dynamics are real—they operate within schools, in ongoing attempts at curricular reform and the redesign of standardized tests, inside political systems, and in attacks on ethnic studies, immigrant rights, voting rights, and language-diverse instruction.

- Recognizing the knowledge students already have as we—teachers, teacher educators, researchers, and others—seek to contribute to it in meaningful ways. As I think more about this statement, I will work at doing a better job of listening to students and including their perspectives inside curricular designs and choices in ways that are critical, meaningful, and purposeful. In other words, I will seek to work with and alongside students in collaborative ways that might create openings for problem-raising, problem-posing, and Democratic Engagements that have implications for activities within, beyond, and outside of school walls.

- Accounting for, and building on, cultural relevancy in our instruction and from students' existing experiences. In commitments to multicultural education and equity pedagogies—which I argue should be the centerpieces of any critical work one does in language, literacy, and culture—it becomes important to employ theories in Culturally Relevant Instruction, Cultural Modeling, and Critical Race Theory. In addition to the work on identity, place, race, and counter-storytelling that can emerge from these theoretical frames, accounting for cultural relevancy in teaching and learning processes has the potential to help teachers and students recognize the rich history of Black and Brown people as readers, writers, inventors, and leaders. Thus, these contributions should become centered in (and central to) teaching and learning.

- Approaching teaching and learning as Projects in Humanization, or PiH (see Kinloch & San Pedro, in progress). Such projects are far-reaching and inclusive of diverse and different voices, perspectives, and ideological and epistemological stances. They are also grounded in a theoretical consideration of listening (Bakhtin, 1981; Bartolome, 1994; Schultz, 2009) as a framework to tell, retell, and re-present stories. Methodologically, such tellings, retellings, and re-presentings occur in nonlinear ways—from left to right, right to left, from conversations on the telephone, via email,

over Skype, and through journaling as essential communicative
forms for teachers and students. Thus, Projects in Humanization
are grounded in a dialogic spiral where teaching, learning, and
researching are central to the relationships and conversations
we construct with others (e.g., colleagues, administrators,
students). Such constructions, then, impact our teaching and
learning experiences and our daily human interactions.

In closing, I recognize that the stories I share in this book are selective
and are smaller parts of larger experiences that occurred with students at
Perennial High School. Clearly, there are many students and literacy engagements that I have not presented here. Nonetheless, I do hope that representative chapters and their respective arguments offer specific insights into the
significance of placing attention on students' literacy practices, challenges,
and engagements. Such a focus can have a major impact on curricular decisions and pedagogical practices within classrooms as well as in efforts
for social justice and democracy in schools and communities. Additionally,
these factors suggest that teachers, teacher educators, researchers, and others who are committed to rich literacy encounters for students—particularly
of color and/or poor and working-class students in public schools—cannot
continue to operate as if the educational, political, and economic landscapes
within this country have not changed. They have changed; therefore, the
ways we work with students must change, too.

Students in the English Course

In the following table, I present the students who were members of the senior-level English course that I taught at Perennial High School. The information below includes students' self-described race or ethnicity, age at the time of the course, and community of residence. For privacy reasons, each student is referred to only by an assigned pseudonym in the table and throughout the entire book.

Students	Self-Described Race or Ethnicity	Age	Community of Residence
Abana	Ghanaian & African American	18	Bronx
Alexandria*	African American	15	Harlem
Aureliano	Hispanic	18	Harlem
Carlos	Hispanic	18	Washington Heights
Celina	Latina	17	Harlem
Christina	African American & Jamaican	19	Harlem
Damya	African American	17	Harlem
Daniel	Hispanic	18	Border: Harlem–Upper West Side
Hector	Hispanic	18	Manhattan/Upper West Side

(continued)

* Alexandria was in 9th grade at the time, but sought permission to register for my senior English course (this was an extra, and not a replacement, course for Alexandria, and in order to receive academic credit, she was required to complete all assignments just like other students).

Jasmine	African American	18	Harlem
Jennifer	Hispanic	17	Harlem
Jose	African American & Puerto Rican	18	Manhattan/ Upper West Side
Juan	Dominican	18	Harlem
Karen	Dominican	17	Manhattan's Morningside Heights
Karimah	African American	17	Harlem's Sugar Hill
Linda	Hispanic	19	Harlem
Mariana	Hispanic	18	Washington Heights
Michael	African American	18	Harlem
Patricia	African American	18	Harlem
Rajon	African American	17	Harlem
Rosa	Puerto Rican (Boricua)**	18	Manhattan/ Upper West Side
Sharif	African American	17	Harlem
Sophie	African American	17	Harlem
Stephen	African American	18	Harlem
Trina	Puerto Rican (Boricua)	18	Spanish Harlem
Victor	Hispanic	17	Bronx
Yvette***	African American	17	Harlem

** According to *Oxford Dictionaries Online*, a Boricua is "a Puerto Rican, especially one living in the United States" (http://oxforddictionaries.com/definition/Boricua?region=us). According to some of my high school students who prefer to be called Boricua, it is a term that signifies ethnic pride, or "valiant people." In various published writings, Boricua is associated with the island, Borinquen, named by Puerto Rico's indigenous Indians, the Taino people.

***Yvette was not a registered student in the class, but used her off/free period to attend nearly all class sessions.

Questions from Pre-Service Teacher Education Candidates to High School Students

Pre-service teacher education candidates at the local university created the following list of questions after the shared class session with students from Perennial High School (see Chapter 1). During my next class session with high school students, I shared these questions with them and, as I discuss in the first chapter in this book, I noticed students reviewing the questions and talking about this shared experience.

1. How can teachers teach students and discuss with them ways to take responsibility for their learning?

2. With all the skills I see as important, real-world skills a student can learn in English class (e.g., how to write well, how to interrogate a text, how to communicate thoughts verbally, how to analyze and respond to ideas), what do you think you should know, need to know, or want to really learn in an English class? (This is based on one high school student's comments that students don't learn what they need to know in their high school classes as they prepare to enter into the real world.)

3. How do students respond to teachers who do not share their racial or ethnic background?

4. One high school student said under her breath (sorry for calling you out) that, referring to teachers contacting parents, "Parents hate it when you do that." Do they? How do you know? What if teachers are calling to share good news? If we should not call parents to stay connected to your outside life, then what should we (teachers) do? What do you think is appropriate and not appropriate for teachers to do without appearing to cause trouble for you or meddle in your life?

5. We talked a lot about getting to know students. How do you want your teachers to know you? Do they see everything you want them

to see and know everything you want them to know? If not, is there something your teachers could do to get to know you better? What can they do to make a better effort? How might you want that to look?

6. Hypothetical: You have a younger brother or sister who is entering high school next year. What would you want most to tell the teachers who will be educating your sibling? What would you want most to tell your brother or sister about the teachers and the school?

7. What is the responsibility of teachers and students to make sure that people are respected culturally and racially and linguistically? How can we all go about taking up this respect in ways that are not superficial?

8. Since there are limited resources and time in the classroom, how can English teachers comment on student writing in ways that build trust, rapport, and a sense of responsibility in the classroom without making students feel as if their writings are not good or that their ideas are not strong? How do you process feedback?

9. Systemic responsibility versus individual responsibility: Kozol focuses on the systemic victimization of the "worse" kids. He rightfully does so! It is a state that we should *not* be in and an unfortunate circumstance. Where and how does personal responsibility for one's education come into play? Can personal responsibility then lead to group collaborations where we all become responsible for the other and the other for ourselves?

10. How do we teach our students that school—the ways they negotiate, advocate, manage, cooperate, rebel, and value themselves, their projects, and their schools as resources and as a community—is preparation for life/for adulthood and the responsibilities that come along with it?

11. We talked about responsibility in the classroom, but to what degree does a teacher have to be responsible for making students want to learn? We can manage classrooms and engage students . . . but what is a teacher's role when students still do not want to learn or when they act like they don't want to learn?

12. What are your ultimate goals in life? Do you know what steps you need to take to reach those goals? Do you have anyone who can help you figure out all of the steps you need to take to be successful in your endeavors?

13. One of the high school students said that the first day of school is really important for setting the *tone* for the year. What are some suggestions for this? What can I do as a high school

teacher on the first day of school to set the tone for a *community* of learners? Also, how do you feel when teachers say that we (the students in the class, the teacher) are a community?

14 If a teacher knows that a student is having difficulties at home (e.g., divorce, little parental support, familial obligations to handle), what can the teacher do to help the student push those issues aside and focus on class? How can a teacher inspire the student to "forget" if even for a short while so that his or her academic life does not suffer? Is it wise to say, "push those issues aside," or do you feel like teachers are trivializing those realities when they say that?

15. How does a teacher gain respect? Is it instant or does it take time?

16. What is the most memorable unit you've studied? Why?

17. What are the ways of building community in the classroom? Have you been surprised by a teacher you thought you did not "vibe" with, but then developed a better relationship? What made the change?

18. Would you feel comfortable bringing in your own questions and thoughts about real-world skills, issues, and knowledge into the classroom? Or would you feel put on the spot if a teacher asks you to do that?

19. What are some of the things you want to ask teachers and want to know about them or even from them?

20. This is a question pre-service teacher education candidates asked me: What are some of the greatest challenges or difficulties you have experienced teaching in such opposite or different atmospheres (a high school with majority students of color in Harlem and a local university with majority White students)?

References

Anderson, J. (1988). *The education of Blacks in the south, 1860–1935.* Chapel Hill: University of North Carolina Press.

Anzaldua, G. (2007). *Borderlands/La Frontera: The new mestiza,* 3rd ed. San Francisco: Aunt Lute Books.

Ayers, W. (1996). A teacher ain't nothin' but a hero: Teachers and teaching in film. In W. Ayers & P. Ford (Eds.), *City kids, city teachers: Reports from the front row* (pp. 228–240). New York: The New Press.

Ayers, W., & Ford, P. (Eds.). (1996). *City kids, city teachers: Reports from the front row.* New York: The New Press.

Bakhtin, M. (1981). *The dialogic imagination* (C. Emerson & M. Holquist, Trans). Austin: University of Texas Press.

Ball, A. (2006). *Multicultural strategies for education and social change: Carriers of the torch in the United States and South Africa.* New York: Teachers College Press.

Ball, A., & Tyson, C. (2011). *Studying diversity in teacher education.* Lanham, MA: Rowman & Littlefield Publishers.

Ball, A. F. (2003). US and South African teachers' developing perspectives on language and literacy: Changing domestic and international roles of linguistic gatekeepers. In S. Makoni, G. Smitherman, A. F. Ball, & A. K. Spears (Eds.), *Black linguistics: Language, society, and politics in Africa and the Americas* (pp. 186–214). London: Routledge.

Banks, C. A. M., & Banks, J. A. (1995). Equity pedagogy: An essential component of multicultural education. *Theory into Practice, 34*(3), 152–158.

Banks, J. A. (Ed). (1996). *Multicultural education, transformative knowledge, and action. Historical and contemporary perspectives.* New York: Teachers College Press.

Barone, D. M. (2004). Case-study research. In N. Duke & M. Mallette (Eds.), *Literacy research methodologies* (pp. 7–27). New York: The Guilford Press.

Bartolome, L. (1994). Beyond the methods fetish: Toward a humanizing pedagogy. *Harvard Educational Review, 62*(2), 173–194.

Bell, C. (2010). *East Harlem revisited.* Mt. Pleasant, SC: Arcadia Publishing.

Berthoff, A. (1987). The teacher as RE-searcher. In D. Goswami & P. Stillman (Eds.), *Reclaiming the classroom: Teacher research as an agency for change* (pp. 28–38). Upper Montclair, NJ: Boynton/Cook.

Brandt, D. (2001). *Literacy in American lives*. Cambridge, UK: Cambridge University Press.

Butchart, R. (1980). *Northern schools, southern Blacks, and reconstruction*. Westport, CT: Greenwood Press.

Butchart, R. (2010). *Schooling the freed people: Teaching, learning and the struggle for Black freedom, 1861–1876*. Chapel Hill: The University of North Carolina Press.

Camangian, P. (2010). Starting with self: Researching autoethnography to foster critically caring literacies. *Research in the Teaching of English, 45*(2), 179–204.

Campano, G. (2007). *Immigrant students and literacy: Reading, writing, and remembering*. New York: Teachers College Press.

Center for Multicultural Education. (2001). *Diversity within unity: Essential principles for teaching and learning in a multicultural society*. Retrieved from http://education.washington.edu/cme/DiversityUnity.pdf

Chapman, T., & Kinloch, V. (2010). Emic perspectives of research. In D. Lapp & D. Fisher (Eds.), *Handbook of research on teaching the English language arts* (pp. 379–385). New York: Routledge.

Cochran-Smith, M., & Lytle, S. L. (1999). The teacher research movement: A decade later. *Educational Researcher, 28*(7), 15–25.

Darling-Hammond, L. (1996). The right to learn and the advancement of teaching: Research, policy, and practice for democratic education. *Educational Researcher, 25*(6), 5–17.

Darling-Hammond, L. (1998). Education for democracy. In W. C. Ayers & J. L. Miller (Eds.), *A light in dark times: Maxine Greene and the unfinished conversation* (pp. 78–91). New York: Teachers College Press.

Darling-Hammond, L. (2010). *The flat world and education: How America's commitment to equity will determine our future*. New York: Teachers College Press & Economic Policy Institute.

Davis, C. T., & Gates, H. L. (1985). *The slave's narrative*. New York: Oxford.

Delpit, L. (1995). *Other people's children: Cultural conflict in the classroom*. New York: The New Press.

Delpit, L. (1996). The politics of teaching literate discourse. In W. Ayers & P. Ford (Eds.), *City kids, city teachers: Reports from the front row* (pp. 194–210). New York: The New Press.

Dimitriadis, G. (2001). "In the clique": Popular culture, constructions of place, and the everyday lives of urban youth. *Anthropology and Education Quarterly, 32*(1), 29–51.

DiPardo, A., Storms, B. A., & Selland, M. (2011). Seeing voices: Assessing writerly stance in the NWP Analytic Writing Continuum. *Assessing Writing*. doi:10.1016/j.asw.2011.01.003

Douglass, F. (2002). *Narrative of the life of Frederick Douglass: An American slave, written by himself*. New York: Bedford/St. Martin's Press. (Original work published 1845)

Du Bois, W. E. B. (Ed.). (1903). *The Negro church*. Atlanta: Atlanta University Press.

Dyson, A. H., & Genishi, C. (2005). *On the case: Approaches to language and literacy research*. New York: Teachers College Press.

Ek, L. D., Machado-Casas, M., Sanchez, P., & Smith, H. (2011). Aprendiendo de sus comunidades/learning from their communities: Bilingual teachers researching urban Latino neighborhoods. In V. Kinloch (Ed.), *Urban literacies: Critical perspectives on language, learning, and community* (pp. 15–37). New York: Teachers College Press.

Fairbanks, C., & Price-Dennis, D. (2011). Studies on popular culture and forms of multimodality. In V. Kinloch (Ed.), *Urban literacies: Critical perspectives on language, learning, and community* (pp. 143–144). New York: Teachers College Press.

Fecho, B. (2004). *"Is this English?" Race, language, and culture in the classroom*. New York: Teachers College Press.

Fisher, M. T. (2004). "The song is unfinished": The new literate and literary and their institutions. *Written Communication 21*(3), 290–312.

Fishman, J., Lunsford, A., McGregor, B., & Otuteye, M. (2005). Performing writing, performing literacy. *College Composition and Communication, 57*(2), 224–252.

Fox, T. (2009). From freedom to manners: African American literacy instruction in the 19th century. In S. Miller (Ed.), *The Norton book of composition studies* (pp. 119–128). New York: W. W. Norton & Company.

The Freedmen's Bureau online. (n.d.). Records of the Bureau of refugees, freedmen and abandoned lands. Retrieved from http://www.freedmensbureau.com/freedmens-bureau

Freire, P. (1973). *Education for critical consciousness*. New York: Seabury Press.

Freire, P. (1997). *Pedagogy of the oppressed*. New York: Continuum. (Original work published 1970)

Gere, A. R. (1994). Kitchen tables and rented rooms: The extracurriculum of composition. *College Composition and Communication, 45*(1), 75–92.

Gilyard, K. (1991). *Voices of the self*. Detroit: Wayne State University.

Ginwright, S. A. (2010). *Black youth rising: Activism & radical healing in urban America*. New York: Teachers College Press.

Greene, M. (2000). *Releasing the imagination: Essays on education, the arts, and social change*. San Francisco: Jossey-Bass.

Gustavson, L. (2008). Influencing pedagogy through the creative practices of youth. In M. L. Hill & L. Vasudevan (Eds.), *Media, learning, and sites of possibilities* (pp. 81–114). New York: Peter Lang.

Haberman, M. (1996). The pedagogy of poverty versus good teaching. In W. Ayers & P. Ford (Eds.), *City kids, city teachers: Reports from the front row* (pp. 118–130). New York: The New Press.

Haddix, M. (2010). No longer on the margins: Researching the hybrid literate identities of Black and Latina preservice teachers. *Research in the Teaching of English, 45*(2), 97–123.

Haddix, M., & Rojas, M. A. (2011). (Re)Framing teaching in urban classrooms: A poststructural (re)reading of critical literacy as curricular and pedagogical practice. In V. Kinloch (Ed.), *Urban literacies: Critical perspectives on language, learning, and community* (pp. 111–124). New York: Teachers College Press.

Haymes, S. (1995). *Race, culture, and the city: A pedagogy for Black urban struggle.* Albany: State University of New York Press.

Hill, M. L. (2009). *Beats, rhymes, and classroom life: Hip-hop pedagogy and the politics of identity.* New York: Teachers College Press.

Holloway, K. (1993). Cultural politics in the academic community: Masking the color line. *College English, 55,* 53–92.

Holt, T. (1990). "Knowledge is power": The Black struggle for literacy. In A. A. Lunsford, H. Moglen, & J. Slevin (Eds.), *The right to literacy* (pp. 91–102). New York: The Modern Language Association of America.

hooks, b. (1989). *Talking back.* Boston: South End Press.

Howard, T. (2010). *Why race and culture matter in schools: Closing the achievement gap in America's classrooms.* New York: Teachers College Press.

Jordan, J. (1996). Nobody mean more to me than you and the future life of Willie Jordan. In W. Ayers & P. Ford (Eds.), *City kids, city teachers: Reports from the front row* (pp. 176–193). New York: The New Press.

Jordan, Z. L. (2011). "Found" literacy partnerships: Service and activism at Spelman College. *Reflections: A Journal of Writing, Service-Learning, and Community Literacy 10*(2), 38–62.

Kim, J. (2011). Is it bigger than hip-hop? Examining the problems and potential of hip-hop in the curriculum. In V. Kinloch (Ed.), *Urban literacies: Critical perspectives on language, learning, and community* (pp. 160–176). New York: Teachers College Press.

Kinloch, V. (2005). Poetry, literacy, and creativity: Fostering effective learning strategies in an urban classroom. *English Education, 37*(2), 96–114.

Kinloch, V. (2007). "The white-ification of the hood": Power, politics, and youth performing narratives of community. *Language Arts, 85*(1), 61–68.

Kinloch, V. (2009). Suspicious spatial distinctions: Literacy research with students across school and community contexts. *Written Communication ,26*(2), 154–182.

Kinloch, V. (2010a). *Harlem on our minds: Place, race, and the literacies of urban youth.* New York: Teachers College Press.

Kinloch, V. (2010b). "To not be a traitor of Black English": Youth perceptions of language rights in an urban context. *Teachers College Record, 112*(1), 103–141.

Kinloch, V. (2011). Crossing boundaries, studying diversity: Lessons from preservice teachers and urban youth. In A. Ball & C. Tyson (Eds.), *Studying diversity in teacher education* (pp. 153–170). Lanham, MD: Rowman & Littlefield Publishers.

Kinloch, V., & San Pedro, T. (in press). The space between listening and story-ing: Foundations for Projects in Humanization (PiH). In D. Paris & M. T. Winn (Eds.), *Humanizing research.* Thousand Oaks, CA: Sage Publications.

Kohl, H. (1991). *I won't learn from you! The role of assent in education*. Minneapolis: Milkweed Editions.

Kozol, J. (2005). *The shame of the nation: The restoration of apartheid schooling in America*. New York: Three Rivers Press.

Ladson-Billings, G. (1994). *The dreamkeepers: Successful teachers of African American children*. San Francisco: Jossey-Bass.

Ladson-Billings, G. (1995). But that's just good teaching! The case for culturally relevant pedagogy. *Theory into Practice, 34*(3), 159–165.

Ladson-Billings, G. (2004). New directions in multicultural education: Complexities, boundaries, and critical race theory. In J. A. Banks & C. A. M. Banks (Eds.), *Handbook of research on multicultural education*, 2nd ed. (pp. 50–68). San Francisco: Jossey-Bass.

Lee, C. D. (1992). Profile of an Independent Black Institution: African-centered education at work. *Journal of Negro Education, 61*(2), 160–177.

Lee, C. D. (2007). *Culture, literacy, and learning: Taking bloom in the midst of the whirlwind*. New York: Teachers College Press.

Lincoln, E., & Mamiya, L. H. (1990). *The Black church in the African American experience*. Durham, NC: Duke University Press.

Lorde, A. (1980). *The cancer journals*. San Francisco: Spinster, Ink.

Mahiri, J., & Sablo, S. (1996). Writing for their lives: The non-school literacy of California's urban African American youth. *Journal of Negro Education, 65*(2), 164–180.

Martinez, R. (2010). Spanglish as literacy tool: Toward an understanding of the potential role of Spanish-English code-switching in the development of academic literacy. *Research in the Teaching of English, 45*(2), 124–149.

Martinez-Roldan, C. M. (2003). Building worlds and identities: A case study of the role of narratives in bilingual literature discussions. *Research in the Teaching of English, 37*, 491–526.

McHenry, E. (2002). *Forgotten readers: Recovering the lost history of African American literary societies*. Durham and London: Duke University Press.

McHenry, E., & Heath, S. B. (1994). The literate and the literary: African Americans as writers and readers—1830–1940. *Written Communication, 11*(4), 419–444.

Michie, G. (2004). *See you when you get there: Teaching for change in urban schools*. New York: Teachers College Press.

Moll, L., & Gonzalez, N. (2001). Lessons from research with language-minority children. In E. Cushman, E. R. Kintgen, B. M. Kroll, & M. Rose (Eds.), *Literacy: A critical sourcebook* (pp. 156–171). Boston: St. Martin's Press.

Mondello, S. (2005). *A Sicilian in East Harlem*. Amherst, NY: Cambria Press.

Moore, J. C. (1997). *The words don't fit in my mouth*. Atlanta: Moore Black Press.

Mora, P. (1986a). Border town: 1938. In P. Mora, *Borders* (p. 68). Houston: Art Publico Press.

Mora, P. (1986b). First love. In P. Mora, *Borders* (p. 68). Houston: Art Publico Press.

Morrison, T. (1970). *The bluest eye*. New York: Holt, Rinehart, & Winston Publishers.

National Association for Multicultural Education. (2003). *Definition of multicultural education.* Retrieved from http://www.nameorg.org/aboutname.html#define.

National Center for Education Statistics. (1999–2000). *School and staffing survey.* Washington, DC: U.S. Department of Education.

National Center on Education and the Economy. (2008). Past examinatons. Retrieved from http://www.nysedregents.org/

Nieto, S., & McDonough, K. (2011). "Placing equity front and center" revisited. In A. F. Ball & C. A. Tyson (Eds.), *Studying diversity in teacher education* (pp. 363–384). Lanham, MA: Rowman & Littlefield Publishers, Inc.

Nino, C. S. (1996). *The constitution of deliberative democracy.* New Haven, CT: Yale University Press.

Noddings, N. (1993). *Educating for intelligent belief or unbelief: The John Dewey lecture.* New York: Teachers College Press.

Noddings, N. (1995). *Philosophy of education.* Boulder, CO: Westview Press.

Pallas, A. M., Natriello, G., & McDill, E. L. (1989). The changing nature of the disadvantaged population: Current dimensions and future trends. *Educational Researcher, 18*(5), 16–22.

Paris, D., & Kirkland, D. E. (2011). "The consciousness of the verbal artist": Understanding vernacular literacies in digital and embodied spaces. In V. Kinloch (Ed.), *Urban literacies: Critical perspectives on language, learning, and community* (pp. 177–194). New York: Teachers College Press.

Perry, T. (2003). Freedom for literacy and literacy for freedom: The African American philosophy of education. In T. Perry, C. Steele, & A. Hilliard III (Eds.), *Young, gifted and Black: Promoting high achievement among African Americans* (pp. 11–51). Boston: Beacon Press.

Pratt, R., & Rittenhouse, G. (Eds.). (1998). *The condition of education, 1998.* Washington, DC: U.S. Government Printing Office.

Rampersad, A. (Ed.). (1995). *The collected poems of Langston Hughes.* New York: Vintage.

Rich, M. F. (2000). America's diversity and growth: Signposts for the 21st century. *Population Bulletin, 55*(2), 1–43. Washington, DC: Population Reference Bureau.

Rodriguez, L. (1996). Always running. In W. Ayers & P. Ford (Eds.), *City kids, city teachers: Reports from the front row* (pp. 11–24) New York: The New Press.

Rothstein, R., Jacobsen, R., & Wilder, T. (2008). *Grading education: Getting accountability right.* New York: Teachers College Press & Economic Policy Institute.

Royster, J. J. (2000). *Traces of a stream: Literacy and social change among African American women.* Pittsburgh: University of Pittsburgh Press.

Schultz, K. (2009). *Rethinking classroom participation: Listening to silent voices.* New York: Teachers College Press.

Sharman, R. L. (2006). *The tenants of East Harlem.* Berkeley: University of California Press.

Shor, I. (1992). *Empowering education: Critical teaching for social change*. Chicago: University of Chicago Press.

Sias, R., & Moss, B. (2011). Rewriting a master narrative: HBCUs and community literacy partnerships: Introduction. *Reflections: A Journal of Writing, Service-Learning, and Community Literacy, 10*(2), 1–15.

Sleeter, C. E. (2005). *Un-standardizing the curriculum: Multicultural teaching in the standards-based classroom*. New York: Teachers College Press.

Souto-Manning, M. (2010). Challenging ethnocentric literacy practices: (Re)positioning home literacies in a Head Start classroom. *Research in the Teaching of English, 45*(2): 150–178.

Souto-Manning, M. (2011). A different kind of teaching: Culture circles as professional development for freedom. In V. Kinloch (Ed.), *Urban literacies: Critical perspectives on language, learning, and community* (pp. 95–110). New York: Teachers College Press.

Stake, R. (2000). Case studies. In N. Denzin & Y. Lincoln (Eds.), *Handbook of qualitative research* (2nd ed., pp. 435–454). Thousand Oaks, CA: Sage Publications.

Staples, J. (2008). "Are we our brothers' keepers": Exploring the social functions of reading in the life of an African American urban adolescent. In M. L. Hill & L. Vasudevan (Eds.), *Media, learning, and sites of possibilities* (pp. 57–72). New York: Peter Lang.

Taylor, M. (2002). *Harlem: Between heaven and hell* Minneapolis: University of Minnesota Press.

Teel, K. M., & Obidah, J. E. (2008). *Building radical and cultural competence in the classroom: Strategies from urban educators*. New York: Teachers College Press.

Torre, M., & Fine, M. (2006). Researching and resisting: Democratic policy research by and for youth. In S. Ginwright, P. Noguera, & J. Cammarota (Eds.), *Beyond resistance! Youth activism and community change: New democratic possibilities for practice and policy for America's youth* (pp. 269–285). New York: Routledge.

Vasudevan, L. (2009). Performing new geographies of literacy teaching and learning. *English Education, 41*(4), 356–374.

Villanueva, V. (1993). *Bootstraps: From an American academic of color*. Urbana, IL: NCTE.

Walker, D. (1969). *Appeal in four articles*. New York: Arno Press. (Original work published 1848)

Willis, A. I., Montavon, M., Hall, H., Hunter, C., Burke, L., & Herrera, A. (2008). *On critically conscious research: Approaches to language and literacy research*. New York: Teachers College Press.

Winn, M. T. (2011). *Girl time: Literacy, justice, and the school-to-prison pipeline*. New York: Teachers College Press.

Witherell, C., & Noddings, N. (1991). *Stories lives tell: Narrative and dialogue in education*. New York: Teachers College Press.

Woodson, C. G. (2011). *Mis-education of the Negro.* New York: Tribeca Books. (Original work published 1933)

X, Malcolm, & Haley, A. (1992). *The autobiography of Malcolm X, as told to Alex Haley.* New York: Ballantine Books. (Original work published 1965)

Yin, R. (1984). *Case study research: Design and methods.* Newbury Park, CA: Sage.

Index

About the Author

Valerie Kinloch is associate professor in literacy studies at The Ohio State University, co-editor of the NCTE/Routledge Book Series in Literacy, and director of the Cultivating New Voices Among Scholars of Color program (CNV). Her research examines literacy engagements and spatial narratives of youth and adults in and out of schools. She is the author of *June Jordan: Her Life and Letters* (2006) and co-editor of *Still Seeking an Attitude: Critical Reflections on the Work of June Jordan* (2004). Valerie's most recent book is an edited collection of critical essays titled *Urban Literacies: Critical Perspectives on Language, Learning and Community* (2011), from which all proceeds and royalties go to support the Cultivating New Voices Among Scholars of Color program. Her book *Harlem on Our Minds: Place, Race, and the Literacies of Urban Youth* received the 2011 Exemplar Research in Teaching and Teacher Education Award from Division K (Teaching & Teacher Education) of the American Educational Research Association (AERA), as well as a 2011 Honorary Mention for Outstanding Research Contribution from Division C (Curriculum Studies) of AERA. In 2010, Valerie was the recipient of the Scholars of Color Early Career Award from AERA and the Dean's Inspiration Award from The Ohio State University. She is a previous recipient of a Spencer Foundation Small Research Grant and a Grant-In-Aid from the National Council of Teachers of English. She is local project director for a national grant-funded project that prepares over 70 K–12 Columbus City Teachers to design and implement high-quality service-learning projects in their schools and local communities alongside students and community organizations. Currently, Valerie is at work on a co-edited book on service-learning in literacy education and on a research project involving educators, students, and community members in South Carolina and in Sierra Leone, West Africa.